FIRST SERVE YOURSELF

FIRST
SERVE
YOURSELF

HOW YOUNG LEADERS AROUND
THE WORLD ARE WINNING
ON THEIR OWN TERMS

VIK KAPOOR

Dan, thanks again!
I cite you breefly at
pg 154 but really your thinking
has made me smarter. And
you gave me an epic cover. VK
Thankyou

NEW DEGREE PRESS

COPYRIGHT © 2021 VIKRAM KAPOOR AND EXTRA-M COACHING
AND CONSULTING, LLC

FIRST SERVE YOURSELF
How Young Leaders Around The World
Are Winning On Their Own Terms

ISBN   978-1-63676-807-6   *Paperback*
          978-1-63730-235-4   *Kindle Ebook*
          978-1-63730-250-7   *Ebook*

Table of Contents for the Active (and Lazy) Reader

---

perhaps more than ever, we are called upon to recognize our vulnerability and be more self-authoring in the design of our lives. Bookshops abound with various approaches to self-help, but one thing that has not been sufficiently recognized is the practice of self-coaching. Vik Kapoor's book fills an important need in our world to engage in a life practice that enhances our inner resourcefulness, enabling us to become better people who can develop the quality of our relationships, and can contribute to creating a better world together." - Alan Sieler, Director, Newfield Institute and author of *Coaching to the Human Soul: Ontological Coaching and Deep Change* Volumes I-IV.

"*First Serve Yourself* is informative and highly practical. Vik offers many ways to coach ourselves, improve our ability to lead, and enhance our quality of life." - Sahil Aneja, author of *Happiology* (which he wrote at age sixteen).

"This book deeply, powerfully, and insightfully describes a new paradigm for coaching. Vikram guides the reader with great detail through the journey in which we can all learn to be our own coaches by "self-coaching." He invites us to literally double the dimensions of improvement that are available to us. The techniques are based on solid scientific research and leverage his international coaching experience, which includes the United Nations. I strongly recommend this book to anyone who takes satisfaction in finding new ways to continuously learn and grow." - Lewis Frees, author of *Align* (in collaboration with Ann Frees).

"Most of the global industry today that is called 'coaching' consists almost entirely of confidence building. But in order to be successful even in building confidence, it is necessary not only to be empathetic and kind, but honest and courageous—especially to oneself. Vikram Kapoor has written a wonderful guide to doing exactly that, exploring the transformational potential of self-coaching, which seeks a middle ground between beating ourselves up and letting ourselves off the hook. Kapoor is immensely experienced and brings an essential cross-cultural dimension to his work. He explores the universal nature of cognitive biases, how they impact our decisions, and what we can do to become more aware of them. His writing is clear, practical, and insightful, and you will walk away with a deeper understanding and more powerful skills, no matter what your occupation or reasons for reading it. It is sure to become a classic in the literature of coaching." - Kenneth Cloke, cofounder of Mediators Beyond Borders (MBBI) and author of *Mediating Dangerously, The Art of Waking People Up* (with Joan Goldsmith) and *The Dance of Opposites.*

This book is for all those who aspire to have an impact in the lives of others, and who realize to do that well, we must first serve ourselves. May you be happy, may you be healthy, may you be at peace and live with ease.

Preface

———

"Know yourself and you will win all battles."

-SUN TZU, THE ART OF WAR

You know we live in serious times, with several major crises all around us, and these moments may well define the next decade or more of our lives.

That's what compelled me to write this self-coaching book, which draws on my experience building coaching programs at the United Nations and my learning from over a hundred leading experts in the field of coaching and professional development.

When you're counting on **you** for that next right answer and the pressure is on, that's when coaching yourself is so important.

ADVICE FROM A COACHING LEGEND

In June 2020, as the COVID-19 pandemic raged around the world, I began using a daily questions activity to help me adjust major areas of my life.

At 9:00 p.m. every night, I asked myself about twenty questions. *Did I do my best to wake up with love in my heart? Did I do my best to meditate for five minutes?* And on and on. I explored things that really matter to me, like health, relationships, meaning, and balance.

Though good daily reminders, after doing this for just **three days**, the list was starting to get exhausting. *Did I do my best to record any learnings from the day? Did I do my best to catch someone doing something right? Did I do my best to choose courage over comfort?*[1]

I struggled with consistency and was feeling depleted, so I had a chat with coaching legend Marshall Goldsmith about it.

If you don't know the name, Marshall Goldsmith is a top global coach of major CEOs, and he has written many key books for executives, including *Triggers, Mojo*, and *What Got You Here Won't Get You There*. I draw on his work all the time, and the man has worked with some of the wealthiest and most powerful people in the world through their defining moments.

---

1   I borrowed this question of choosing "courage over comfort" from vulnerability expert Brené Brown because it forces me to question whether I am avoiding any of the tough stuff in my life. Brené Brown, "Courage Over Comfort: Rumbling with Shame, Accountability, and Failure at Work," *Brené Brown* (blog), March 13, 2018.

I figured my plea for help would earn me a nugget of wisdom.

After all, he popularized this daily questions practice, which he adapted from Benjamin Franklin's early work on virtues. Marshall has been answering his own daily questions "almost every day" for several decades, while most people quit within fourteen days. This man has conquered this self-coaching tool himself, so I settled in to receive his sage words about my feeling depleted.

"Depleted? Yeah, I think that's bullshit," he said.

"Bullshit?" I asked faintly. I was sitting tall in my father-in-law's study and could feel my shoulders suddenly fold inward around my cellphone, as if I had just imploded.

"Bullshit," he replied cheerily. "You aren't depleted from answering your questions because that takes less than three minutes. You're depleted by the existential reality that you have failed at your own priorities."

You see, when you are grading yourself against your own rubric, you cannot blame the fool who wrote the score sheet. You cannot argue with the wording or question its importance. The accountability starts and ends with the person in the mirror.

This is the true power of coaching through self-coaching. You make the rules, you set the standards, and you do the hard work in furthering the meaningful goals you set for yourself. When all is said and done, it is an inside job, with supplemental support.

Marshall told me he has his illustrious clients meet in circles every week to talk about their daily questions. *Did people try their best to set clear goals this week? Did they do their best to be happy?*

Two surprisingly difficult questions to score well on every day, even for our best and brightest.

Inspired by his stories, and his assertion that we (himself included) are "cowardly, undisciplined, and in need of help," I doubled down on my own daily questions practice by hiring a personal assistant to call me every day, which has made all the difference.

But before I get too far ahead of myself, let's cover the basics.

THE COACHING SPACE

More and more people every year are waking up to the tremendous advantage of professional coaching, but it is still not a fully mainstream service.[2] Senior leaders and CEOs are keen on having a personal coach, even really depending on them, but many people—young leaders especially—believe either they cannot afford one or do not need one. This book addresses these concerns by helping you build an enhanced toolkit for coaching yourself and integrating and harnessing the impact of supplemental coaching.

---

2   *2020 ICF Global Coaching Study: Executive Summary* (Lexington, KY: International Coach Federation, 2020).

IT'S THE MANAGER

Gallup's book *It's the Manager* makes clear the mid-level manager will be the deciding factor in the success of enterprise in the coming years. To be effective, Gallup says, these managers must learn to be good coaches.[3] But what does that even mean? My research has shown **these very managers do not fully understand coaching.** They do not see its value because they have not had the proper exposure, and as a result, they cannot be good coaches themselves.

By coaching yourself, you can learn to work with new mindsets and create best practices for coaching your colleagues and teams, which will set you up to be a really good manager. Those skills go back home with you as well, and also serve your family and community.

MY JOURNEY AS A COACH

I have been fortunate to help create and run coaching programs in over forty countries for the United Nations (UN Development Programme, UN Women, and the UN Population Fund) while also maintaining a portfolio of private coaching clients on six continents.

Earlier in life, I was a class action attorney—an advocate who spent a fair amount of time in court and advising my disadvantaged clients on what to do. When it was time to decide whether to settle the case or keep fighting, however, I found I needed to shift into more of a coach-like approach, asking clients about their needs, their values, their well-being, and

---

3   Jim Clifton and Jim Harter, *It's the Manager: Moving from Boss to Coach* (New York: Gallup Press, 2019), 186.

how they balance priorities in life. This was my first taste of how coaching can help.

When I got to the US Federal Emergency Management Agency (FEMA) as a conflict resolution expert, I quickly realized how powerful coaching could be. Employees who thought they were being harassed or who found themselves in lingering conflict with managers or peers oftentimes had more complex needs, and the rules did not neatly answer all their questions.

After seeing the tremendous value of coaching, I decided to launch a coaching company to amplify the impact of millennial leaders. That practice grew to include ambassadors-in-training, members of the United States Special Forces, leaders at top technology companies and a range of amazing people leading change around the world.

This book cherry-picks my favorite coaching tools from all those interactions so it can serve as a foundation for your own exploration as well. It's a book I wish I had even ten years ago.

THE PROBLEM WITH ADVICE

The problem with advice is it is subjective and therefore biased, and this bias is amplified when the advisor does not have enough information. Oftentimes when we are giving our friends, kids, or parents advice, we are doing so with incomplete information. Most of the time, we do not even know what the real problem is, but this does not stop us at all! We obviously know something, and we do not hesitate to share it.[4]

I am sure you will need more convincing of this idea, but I invite you to think about it. It is just too much a part of our DNA to give advice. We enjoy it, and our ability to give advice is often perceived as a demonstration of the value we add to the world around us. A common complaint I got from my coaches in East Africa and the Middle East was "why on Earth would someone come to me with their problem if I cannot give them the answer?"

Coaching is about changing this perspective and adjusting our beliefs so we are not rescuing people, but rather partnering with them to find truly valuable solutions that actually work.

THE (NOT SO) BIG IDEA

In many key moments, we can coach ourselves—whether it be about fear, anger, lack of clarity in decision-making, bad habits, or something confusing, there are ways to make a difference for yourself.

This book invites you to build your own approach from a menu of powerful tools, frameworks, and resources (and encourages you to go out and find others for your unique context). If you remain curious and flexible with yourself, you can do a lot with self-coaching.

---

4   Michael Bungay Stanier, "How to tame your Advice Monster," filmed February 2020 at TEDxUniversityofNevada, Reno, Nevada, video, 14:29.

In this book, you will:

- Learn from cutting edge neuroscience research on what impacts your behavior and reactions, as well as your ability to set and achieve commitments
- Discover ways to figure out your values and strengths so you can build your own personal mission statement to guide you in your career
- Create your very own custom action plan for success in your life and a basic resilience plan
- See how self-coaching tools and techniques apply in practice to help us improve our lives, shift gears, pick up positive habits, or launch into something bigger

THIS IS FOR YOU!

With all this in mind, this book is for managers, coaches, parents, entrepreneurs, and all those who want to improve or refresh their lives in meaningful ways. It is also a great supplement to formal coaching, therapy, and mentoring.

Join us online when you begin implementing these tools! We are doing it together.

Vikram Kapoor, 2021
Falls Church, Virginia (USA)

> *Christopher Robin to Pooh: "Promise me you'll always remember: You're braver than you believe, and stronger than you seem, and smarter than you think."*
>
> *-A. A. MILNE*

PART I

SETTING THE STAGE FOR SELF-REFLECTION

"Success is getting what you want. Happiness is wanting what you get."

-DALE CARNEGIE

You can think of self-reflection like an excavation or grand exploration.

Through critical self-reflection, we serve ourselves by deepening our self-awareness. Organizational psychologist Tasha Eurich has called this "the meta skill of the 21st century" because other qualities deemed essential for success such as "emotional intelligence, empathy, influence, persuasion, communication, and collaboration all stem from self-awareness."[5]

You can coach yourself to success once you have landed on a suitable target, and it all begins with self-awareness. What does success or "winning" even mean to you? This is the underlying question for this book and something we will come back to again. Are you trying to be rich and famous? Do you want a lot of free time to spend with family? Do you have a deep interest in social causes or traveling or sports?

Two Key Requests

You will see these shaded boxes at times to illustrate key points and share stories of how concepts come together through real examples. There will be vignettes from high-potential young leaders, perhaps just like you, who are winning in life through self-coaching. Their messages are a source of inspiration, and I invite you to "trust your gut" as you figure out what tools will work best for you.

There are two primary requests for success ahead. Neither is simple nor easy, but they are essential, and we will all have to work at them to optimize our results.

---

5   Tasha Eurich, *Insight* (New York: Crown Business, 2017), 5.

Compassionate Self-Listening.[6]
When you **listen to yourself** as you read this book, my ask is that you be as compassionate as possible. You are your own best friend. Hear yourself out to ensure the self-coaching continues. Curiosity is one of the greatest ways to show compassion. To be clear, we are not talking about tough love here. Anger, disgust, disdain, sarcasm, repulsion, exasperation, cussing at yourself, eye-rolling— none of this is compassion. You get the idea, I hope.

Humble Self-Inquiry.[7]
Any great coach will tell you the **art of inquiry is a super-power.** The type, tone, and timing of questions also matter. Humble self-inquiry means asking yourself questions you do not really have the answer to...yet, and this kind of inquiry is both non-leading and non-judgmental. You will practice this throughout the book by going deeper and continuing to question the root of particular thoughts and emotions that come up.

When you listen with compassion, you get to better questions, and when you ask better questions, you ought to listen more compassionately. These two work together to help you make the most of this investment in yourself.

---

6   Though the concept is not novel, I credit its adaptation from Chade-Meng Tan, whose work introduced me to the phrase "compassionate listening," in the *Search Inside Yourself* workshop series, "Search Inside Yourself Program," Search Inside Yourself Leadership Institute, accessed March 12, 2021.

7   I credit Edgar Schein's work *Humble Inquiry* for the basis of this guideline. Edgar H. Schein, *Humble Inquiry: The Gentle Art of Asking Instead of Telling* (San Francisco, CA: Berrett-Koehler Publishers, 2013), passim.

CHAPTER 1

Positive Intentions
Beat Skepticism

———

"Progress isn't achieved by preachers or guardians of moral-
ity, but by madmen, hermits, heretics, dreamers, rebels, and
skeptics."

-STEPHEN FRY

A few years ago, my boss very sweetly asked if I could do a talk at the headquarters of the US Federal Bureau of Investigation (FBI) in Washington, DC. "Could you go talk to the FBI? They want something interesting on conflict resolution."

Spouting off something at the historic Hoover Building wasn't exactly in the "comfort zone" category for me, but she talked me up like she did for everyone on the team ("I am sending you one of our best") and I hated to let her down, so I went with a smile and a gulp.

I figured I could manage a small group of maybe thirty to fifty people like my usual audiences at the time, even if some of them were a little secretive or "stiff." I was secretly picturing characters from *Men in Black* in my audience, so I took my classic Ray-Ban Wayfarers in case there was a group picture.

I was very surprised as I walked into the auditorium at the FBI building to find over four hundred people in the room and another five hundred plus on live telecast. Almost *one thousand people?* Could you imagine me totally bombing this one? I pictured it vividly in that moment.

Sweat pouring down my back. Gulping down four bottles of water in a flash of a second. People walking out mid-way during one of my many long pauses as I gather my thoughts. I was surprised at how fast my brain could conjure up that cheery chain of events. In this parallel reality, I totally choked.

All of that flashed before my eyes before I took a breath. And here was my response. *Almost one thousand people. Awesome, how exciting.* Images of Winnie the Pooh and playful Tigger. Memories of award-winning Model United Nations debates. Breathing out longer than I breathe in to reset my nervous system. Going to the balcony in my mind to add perspective. Forcing a huge (feigned) smile for my hundreds of new friends in the audience.

Drawing on my personal coaching toolkit I will share with you in this book, I reoriented myself and delivered the talk that actually launched my global speaking career. What does Tigger have to do with it? Positive anchoring to a playful image can help, and I will explain more later.

I have gone to other exciting venues like the White House Executive Office Building, the US Marine Corp Base at Quantico, and the United Nations headquarters in New York and Nairobi, among others, but nothing compares to that first talk at the FBI Hoover Building on "Dialing Down the Drama."

I should say the certificate I earned from the FBI that day is signed by none other than former FBI director James Comey. Just three weeks later, he was fired from his senior role by tweet, which led to the appointment of a special counsel, a year-long investigation ("the Mueller investigation"), and the first Trump impeachment trial, all of which will go down in US history as a fairly "dramatic" time to be in federal government service. I had no way of knowing how relevant my talk was that day. In the weeks to come, I got a number of questions from those participants about how to "dial down the drama" in their lives. So, you never know how these tools will help shape you and your audience, but they may have a lasting effect far beyond what you can imagine!

One of the bedrock concepts in that training and in this book is when it comes to any major life decision or event, you want to start with an intention. What is your intention? Is it to be sad or angry? These would be perfectly reasonable responses for the audience at the time. Is it to punch back? Is it to find work elsewhere, or to become actively disengaged from work? Is it to accept and move on?

Our intention is a guidepost for our logical brain, and it gives us the grounding we need when the emotional brain gets excited or agitated. In key instances, intention can be the difference between life and death, employment and unemployment, a happy marriage and divorce, or addiction and recovery.

In fact, Caroline Webb in *How to Have a Good Day* scours the research and concludes setting daily intentions can have profound positive impact on mood, productivity, and overall success on a day-by-day basis.[8] Setting good intentions can be a big deal, and often transformative. I have seen it myself.

HOW HARD IS IT REALLY TO SET DAILY INTENTIONS?

When we talk about transformative things, the shift takes real work, energy, and commitment. If your intention is to make it to the finish line and really stretch in the process, nothing can stop you.

> **Young Leader Profile: Karim's Practice Makes Perfect**
>
> Karim Abouelnaga was named on the *Forbes* 30 under 30 list in Education and is a former World Economic Forum Global Shaper. He is CEO of Practice Makes Perfect and the author of two books, including *The Purpose-Driven Social Entrepreneur*. Karim's mission is to improve the public education system, and he has been spreading his message as a TED Fellow. Karim moves fast and he has

---

8   Caroline Webb, *How to Have a Good Day* (New York: Crown Business, 2016), 37-46.

enjoyed the benefit of coaching during many prestigious fellowships.

He uses what he learned to coach himself and his team, and he is particularly focused on meditation and mindfulness. "I've meditated for five to ten minutes a day every morning for the last eight years, and when I pull back or miss a day, I notice." Karim also does a gratitude meditation every Friday, and he incorporates mindfulness into the workplace by starting each team meeting with three deep breaths. "Folks just do it now." He feels that slowing down with mindfulness for a few minutes actually allows him to be just as effective without feeling like he's pushing on the pedal as much as he used to.

How did he get to his practice? "The same way I do everything. I start by copying what someone else says works, and I do it for a while until I understand why it works, and then I customize it to work better for me."

HOW TO READ THIS BOOK
Many authors over the years have given their readers some hints on how to read their book. In the 1940s, the executive editor of the Encyclopedia Britannica (and his colleague) wrote a book called *How to Read a Book*.

The art of reading, they explain, is "the process whereby a mind, with nothing to operate on but the symbols of the readable matter...elevates itself by the power of its own operations. The mind passes from understanding less to understanding more."[9]

For your mind to do that, you will need to really engage the content and make it your own. It will be critical for you to be an active reader here. Challenge assumptions, test things out, and see what works for you.

One other thing they mention—you can be critical and challenge the content, but you can only legitimately do so once you have *understood* the content. So, once you get what I am saying here, then and only then should you really engage in the thought process of "I agree, I disagree, or I suspend judgment."[10]

I am not surprised if you are skeptical of the concept of "self-coaching." After all, there are no limits to self-help resources out there. This kind of mental resistance is, in fact, healthy and meaningful. It will keep you sharp and allow you to discern what will work well for you.

The skepticism also might get in our way in this book, just as it might get in our way in life. Striking the balance for a certain "healthy skepticism" will be important. We all have this assessment mechanism, to "size people up" and determine whether something is worth our time and energy.

---

9   Mortimer Adler and Charles Van Doren, *How to Read a Book* (New York: Simon and Schuster, 2014), 8.

10   Ibid. (on the importance of suspending judgment).

You can begin by looking at your own "Inner Critic" or "Assessor." Oftentimes, dealing with that aspect of us will be key to success in any number of goals we set. In coaching, we say "suspend disbelief" or "put your Assessor away."

Where self-coaching is concerned, please go for it, and resist the urge to sabotage yourself. I challenge you to thank that sabotage voice and put it away, because you've already made the decision this quest is worth at least a little bit of your time and energy right now.

I look at it like **"grounded hope,"** defined as "a realistic view of the situation plus a strong view of one's ability to control one's destiny through one's efforts."[11] You hope for something good here, and you've grounded that hope in a way that makes it practical and attainable. We need to aspire to something we have control over, with some real limits.

Knowing yourself and your "edge" or what's a "good stretch" will be especially important as you flip through this book. The "edge" is both a physical sensation (as in yoga) and a metaphor; what is not too little and not too much, but a good push. As my yoga teacher and wellness coach Linda Baron says, "In exploring the edge, we can learn how much safety we need to protect ourselves and how much discomfort we can tolerate to grow. It may be metaphorically similar to the idea of leaning into conflict—pushing through the comfort zone." Please keep looking for that edge if you can, because

---

11   David B. Feldman and Lee Daniel Kravetz, *Supersurvivors* (New York: HarperCollins Publishers Inc, 2014), 43.

that awareness both helps us grow **and** keeps us from burning out.

There are a few more things you should keep in mind while reading, adapted from Adler and Van Doren:

1. Read the table of contents and dive in where you find value.
2. Look at the young leader profiles in each chapter to get clear about what can help you.
3. Engage the reflection questions at the end of each segment.
4. Do the exercises that resonate for you. It's okay if something does not work for you; maybe you can adapt it.
5. Take notes in the margins, or underline/circle/highlight things that resonate.
6. Create or join an online implementation group.
7. Reach out to my team if we can serve your learning or self-coaching journey.

The best reading demands active participation, so make it a contact sport and you will create a great deal of value for yourself.

To put a finer point on this, practical books such as this one do not actually solve the practical problems they are discussing. Only your action can solve and address the issues in your life, and this book can only help you to create the means to make moves in that positive direction.[12]

---

12   Adler and Van Doren, *How to Read a Book*, 189.

The Wisdom of Permission from a Master Coach

Cecilia Schrijver is one of two International Coaching Federation (ICF) Master Certified Coaches (MCC) in the Philippines, as well as the managing partner of Haraya Coaching and director of training for Coach Masters Academy. As a Certified Daring Way™ Facilitator, she draws heavily on the work of Dr. Brené Brown on vulnerability, shame, and courage. Cecilia often introduces the "Permission Slips" tool to her clients when they embark on something new, challenging, or vulnerable. "What do we need to give ourselves permission to do? Permission to fail, to feel disappointed, to cry, to succeed, or to 'feel all the feeling' in a particular moment?"

Cecilia appreciates the self-coaching tools in this book and invites readers to set an intention "to go deep and to get real." The techniques will not have the desired impact unless we give ourselves permission to take an honest and non-judgmental look at ourselves.

Our wisdom lies in our ability to reflect with authenticity and commitment to embrace the messiness of our own lives. "How honest are you being in your journal, with your own thoughts, wants, triggers, and desires? What clarity, learning, or insight is available to you?"

In order to get the most out of the self-coaching tools here, what is it you need to give yourself permission for?

WHAT EXACTLY IS COACHING?

Most people do not fully understand the concept of professional coaching. I could write a book about the theory and its evolution, but only a few nice nerds would ever read it. To keep it simple, there are sports coaches, advisors, mentors, consultants, and therapists, and then there are professional coaches.

We are talking about coaching in the professional coaching context, which is a process that puts the client in the driver's seat to figure out what is going to work best for them. There is much less telling and much more asking.

We do it this way because the neuroscience research teaches us that if I give you an answer, the odds of it being the right answer and you executing on it are quite low, but if you come up with your own answer, the odds of you executing on it are high. This is intuitively about autonomy, choice, and expertise. After all, you are the expert in your life. The coach can only share what might work for others and it's your job to apply that to your reality.

Here is a basic example. If you ask for help with managing stress during the unprecedented COVID-19 crisis, a coach will ask you to talk more about what you hope to gain out of the coaching conversation. It might go something like this:

Coach - So, what brings you here today?

Client - I am stressed during this pandemic and want some advice.

Coach - I can certainly understand the stress. What makes this topic important to you right now?

Client - Unless I can manage my stress, my health will deteriorate and my relationships might unravel. It is taking a serious toll on my life.

Coach - Thank you for sharing that important information, and I can understand anyone in your shoes might be feeling this way. What can we accomplish during our thirty minutes together today?

Client - I have no idea. I was hoping to talk about it and get your advice.

Coach - Many clients think about the outcome of the conversation to ground them in this time with me. It helps us to keep moving toward an objective of your choosing. You might say you want to assess an issue and get more clarity, or you may want a specific game plan, or an immediate next step, a new perspective on an issue, or some resources, or maybe something else?

Client - I think for today I want to assess and explore what is happening, to determine one meaningful next step I can take this week to reduce the stress.

A good coach would walk you through your focus and outcome in this way so you have a roadmap you are co-creating with the coach. You do not want to be in a situation where the back-and-forth is authoritative, directive, and overly advisory because it cuts against the science and practice of coaching that makes the process so powerful.

If we wanted advice, there is no absence of free advice out there. Ask your friends and family, or the stranger sitting next to you on the plane or bus. They all have something to share, but that is not coaching. There is an old saying, "If you can tell the difference between good advice and bad advice, you don't need advice."

Many years ago, I met Frank, who had some anxiety about sweating on stage during performances. He was worried his perspiration would get in the way of his ability to perform well, so he consulted a friend who was a coach. Frank's friend quickly slipped into advisor mode and told him all about her own experiences, the professionals he could consult, including a therapist, and she suggested he try zinc supplements and a breathing exercise. Frank recalled walking away from that conversation in a daze, feeling lost and almost like a patient who had left urgent care with confusion about his next steps. His sweating persisted for some time until he got the right help to address it.

What Frank's friend provided him was most certainly not coaching, but many people expect a lot of advice from a coach, and then they get a lot of advice that is just not all that helpful.

WHAT IS SELF-COACHING?

When you talk to yourself, is it with generosity, gratitude, compassion, and support? Is there curiosity and dialogue, or is it directive? If you are like most people, you spend most of your time criticizing, blaming, regretting, wondering, doubting, wishing, and demanding. *Why can't I do this? What's wrong with me? I used to be better at this, but I've forgotten it now. How could I have let myself forget?*

Okay, get up, it's time to hit the gym, you can do it.

Calm down, it's just a presentation, no big deal.

None of this is actually coaching yourself, sadly.

Coaching yourself introduces curiosity in the form of gentle and humble inquiry, thereby building structures that work for you in ways that allow you to be your best with a smile.

It's about self-compassion, resilience, and transformation through experimentation, iteration, and learning.

This book is packed with real-life examples and hard science to get you thinking differently about your life and your future. I make it "snackable" so you can dive right in and start making meaningful adjustments.

You will get the hang of it and start implementing more tools and techniques that work in your life.

You don't win any awards for taking on too much at once!

As you start to experience success, please share with your colleagues, teams, families, and the wider world. Your effort is contagious and makes a difference.

Young Leader Profile: Jaclyn Powers Through

Jaclyn DiGregorio is a two-time best-selling author, motivational speaker, and life coach for young women. Her TEDxYouth Talk speaks to the power of intention, as she recounts the story of running a marathon on a stress fracture, and how she almost gave up at mile twelve. "I had an idea," she explains. "What if I just took the next step...and what if after that I just took one more step? I began repeating the mantra 'one foot in front of the other'...where each word became another step."[13] Sure enough, she finished the twenty-six miles.

To Jaclyn, the only way to become a good coach and leader is to invest in coaching yourself every day. "I practically coach myself 40 percent of the day," she explained to me over our video meeting. "It's about questioning your limiting beliefs, journaling and meditating about them, and listening to the words you say to yourself and to the people around you."

When you pile on the intention and reinforce your belief in yourself, you build the courage needed to do hard things.

---

13   *TEDx Talks*, "The Simple Formula that Builds Courage | Jaclyn DiGregorio | TEDxYouth@Berwyn," October 26, 2020, video, 13:02.

YOUR TURN

1. What is your intention in reading this book? Is it to just skim through it and put it aside, or is it to delve in and make it a part of your life? Get ready to be amazed...

2. Are you committed to practicing compassionate self-listening and humble self-inquiry? How will you remind yourself to do so?

"Some books are to be tasted, others to be swallowed, and some few to be chewed and digested."

-*FRANCIS BACON*

CHAPTER 2

It's Confusing Being Human: A Primer

"It is the mark of an educated mind to be able to entertain a thought without accepting it."

-ARISTOTLE

Managers are failing in organizations. Many parents are barely hanging on at home. People are overwhelmed, more anxious than ever, and generally struggling to tread water amidst global crises. The more we know about being human, the more confusing and complicated it seems to become.

We live in this VUCA world, right? Volatile. Uncertain. Complex. Ambiguous.[14] There is no other way to describe a

---

14 General Thurman characterized the strategic leadership environment in terms of volatility, uncertainty, complexity, and ambiguity. Maxwell P. Thurman, "Strategic Leadership" (presentation, The Strategic Leadership Conference, US Army War College, Carlisle Barracks, PA, 11 February 1991), cited in Richard H. Mackey, Sr., *Translating Vision into Reality:*

decade that saw a global pandemic and the widespread displacement of people around the world, among other major crises and tragedies. Time and resources are limited, burnout is real, and assaults on mental health are up. I have personally seen many (even very high-performing) people are having breakdowns like never before, and civil unrest is also sadly increasing in different parts of the world.

Aren't you happy you joined me for this cheerful check-in?

Things will regularly change, our identity will change, and we will want to be (or will be forced to be) different as we grow and evolve. How this process unfolds—and how to navigate it, from vision to action—can shed light on the best available resources and how to acquire them.

Coaching yourself can be a powerful competitive advantage as you find your unique gift to the world and begin to give it away. But before you can do that, you must first navigate the complexities of what makes it so confusing to be human. This chapter sets the foundation for the behavioral science we will be using throughout the book.

HITCHING A RIDE

The woman in my car was screaming very loudly. Understandably so, because we were careening around a corner, skidding ever faster toward the concrete holding wall, tires squealing. That much noise and the smell of burning rubber

---

The Role of the Strategic Leader (Carlisle Barracks, PA: US Army War College, 1992), 10.

would be troubling for anyone, but the driver hadn't yet seemed to notice.

"Ahhhhhhhhhhhhhhh," my teammate Michelle continued afresh, and I could hear the raw terror loud and clear. Surely, the driver was hearing this, too, but nothing would distract him from his mission, and so far, that mission clearly had no need for the brakes!

Or maybe the brakes had failed? The driver pretended like we weren't even there, and that worried me most.

I met this man just minutes ago, and he invited me into his car very hurriedly. He said maybe two words to me and with a quick "enchanté," we were off in a rush.

I'd seen movies like this that ended very badly. *A dumb move by a dumb American*, I thought to myself. *Did I just get in the car with a French Tyler Durden? Is this how it was going to end for me?* I took a sharp breath and did a little chant under my breath.

This driver was going way too fast into that turn, and now I felt like we were flying through the air, bouncing on the asphalt in the unnatural way they sometimes show in cartoons. Time slowed down.

I'd never experienced someone driving like this before, and just as I summoned the courage and breath to object, we evened out. I did a sharp exhale, and without any hesitation at all, the driver did something with the clutch and then went pedal to the metal to accelerate to one hundred twenty kilometers an hour flat out.

Why are we accelerating so fast? So it wasn't an accident? My brain was moving very slowly and my body just wanted to jump out of the car if it weren't going so bloody fast. *Wasn't there a grisly Tarantino movie about something like this, with a stunt car?*

I was stuck in this car with this crazy person and a screamer. What to do?

I almost bit through my tongue as we bent into another turn, followed by more skidding, skidding, skidding, the strong smell of burning rubber, and continued screaming from our frantic other passenger, like clockwork.

We were at the world-famous *Le Mans* racetrack in the South of France and this went on for a few more minutes. Michelle never really stopped screaming, and I stumbled out of the car when it was over, my legs like jelly. I wasn't even the driver and my adrenals felt shot for the day.

I could feel something was different when we arrived at the racetrack because we were immediately ushered into the control room. That's the fancy room with all the cameras and consoles, and it was only us and the staff. I was in town for a Rotary International exchange and a director of the race happened to be a Rotarian. He was a nice guy and very generous with his time to show us around the facility, where we saw some fancy race cars like McLarens and took cool pictures. Score!

The next thing I knew, the track's Audi pace car had pulled up and the driver was motioning. *You want me to hop in?* I did the silly thing of looking around to make sure a bona fide celebrity was not standing behind me. Silly because obviously no one would just be *standing around* on *Le Mans* racetrack.

At age twenty-five, I was the youngest member of this Rotary vocational exchange to the gorgeous Loire Valley of France, and as the chef de l'équipe (Team Leader), I was the guinea pig with many opportunities to practice my courage. "The Team Leader will try the foie gras first." That meant I jumped into the car first, too, and I innocently thought we were taking a nice pace lap around the track. You can imagine my surprise.

Let me unpack what happened in this story above and why it matters to you.

COGNITIVE BIASES ABOUND
At the outset, let us be clear that you and I have cognitive biases. Did you assume we were drifting on a racetrack or did you think something worse was happening? We are in many ways reliant on our brains to process information for us in one direction or another—either confirm what I already know, or discard and diminish the conflicting data. This is called confirmation bias and selective perception. Our biases are based on our models of the world, and we are able to examine and influence those models. Understanding explicit and implicit bias is so important I devote a later chapter to it.

LOGIC AND EMOTION: THE ELEPHANT AND THE RIDER

As a helpful analogy, think of your brain as split into two entities: logic and emotion. The emotional brain is an elephant and the logical brain is the rider of this elephant. When the rider is having a good day (the logic is sound) and the elephant is cooperative (stable emotions, no agitation or excitement), the rider has no problem maneuvering the elephant. But when the elephant is agitated or aroused, that rider starts to run into some serious trouble.[15]

Maybe you've never ridden an elephant before and so this is less easy to grasp tangibly, but perhaps you've ridden a horse or a camel, or you've been in a snowstorm when your car began to skid a bit. Let's just say any minor movements can have very major implications. This is important because many of us believe our logical tendencies are in complete control.

At *Le Mans*, my elephant brain was very agitated and was signaling for me to jump out of the car, but the rider quickly pulled me back to reality.

If you've ever tried quitting cigarettes or dieting, you may have intuitively learned of the power of the elephantine "emotional brain" at its worst, and the possible struggle between elephant and rider. This is why we need structure in our lives, whether it be calendar reminders, communities to help us with our goals, or any number of other tools and techniques that will be covered in this book.

---

15   Jonathan Haidt, *The Happiness Hypothesis: Putting Ancient Wisdom to the Test of Modern Science* (New York: Basic Books, 2006), 3.

Much of what we must do is to notice the elephant, remember the power dynamics involved, and give the rider as much leverage as possible in key moments, while taking the time to really listen to the elephant and its concerns as well. Sometimes the elephant gives us critical information that can protect our interests and livelihoods. Ultimately, we also need to honor and respect both rider and elephant are limited and may steer us awry from time to time. Giving ourselves grace and acting with self-compassion will be key in the journey to self-coaching mastery.

SURVIVE-THRIVE DICHOTOMY IS HARDWIRED

According to brain researcher Lisa Ann Barrett, our brain is optimizing itself solely to help keep the body alive, and that is its key focus.[16] If our brain's only real function is indeed to keep our body alive, then the critical role of the survive-thrive dichotomy for our nervous system becomes even more obvious.

You are generally in one of two states—what psychologist and coach Daniel Ellenberg has referred to as "survive mode" and "thrive mode." If you are in survive mode, you are working hard to tread water, continually scanning your environment for danger, and interpreting things as if they may be hostile or limiting. If you are in thrive mode, you are drawing inspiration from the environment, feeling hopeful, and experiencing demonstrable support from others.

This "defend/discover" axis as described by Caroline Webb in *How to Have a Good Day,* is a linear spectrum, from defensive

16   Ibid., 10–11.

mode on one end to discovery mode on the other.[17] Webb teaches us about the sheer amount of effort the brain spends to protect us from immediate dangers, and how this can wreak havoc on our day-to-day judgment. *Is this person trying to help me or hurt me?* is a question that might be going on in your brain more often than you realize.

Antidotes to this excessive worrying are to notice you are in defensive mode, to use (or appreciate) humor in tense situations, and to find ways to reward yourself either by refocusing on your autonomy and intrinsic motivation or by learning something new that excites you.

At *Le Mans*, I tried to shake off the screaming with a little encouragement to Michelle and a smile or nod to the driver, but they were both understandably busy (screaming and driving, respectively). I did find solace in focusing in on the dashboard and the nuances of timing around the track, in the hopes that I could learn something that would distract from the reality of the situation, but my body definitely was feeling under attack.

POLYVAGAL THEORY SHOWS ADDITIONAL COMPLEXITY OF THE NERVOUS SYSTEM

Survival mode is also key to the polyvagal theory (PVT), which is a compelling way of looking at your nervous system's response to danger. Under PVT, there are two vagus nerves in the body, which regulate things like breathing and heart rate.

---

17   Caroline Webb, *How to Have A Good Day: A Revolutionary Handbook for Work and Life* (New York: Crown, 2016), 20–27.

When you apply the science to practice, think of it like a ladder with three rungs—the top, middle, and bottom of the ladder.[18]

The top of the ladder is ventral vagal, or the ideal state. Here you are feeling supported, calm, at ease even if alert, and in a place of tranquility even if there is activity. You exhibit a low heart rate and subdued endocrine response.[19] You experience a sense of peace, like when in deep meditation.

The middle of the ladder is your sympathetic response—adrenaline, mild sweating, perhaps a dry throat. There is a gradient here—a little edginess, which can grow to higher levels of stress and panic. This is the phase you are in when you are leading a stressful meeting or delivering an important speech.

The bottom of the ladder is dorsal vagal, which is demonstrated with a kind of overwhelm, or shut down, and it might feel like a release of some kind. You are feeling relaxed but not because you went up to ventral vagal and are at ease; rather, you went down to dorsal vagal and are in a shutdown mode.[20]

---

18 Deb Dana, *Polyvagal Theory: Using the Autonomic Ladder to Work with Perfectionism* (Mansfield, CT: The National Institute for the Clinical Application of Behavioral Medicine, 2018).

19 Ibid.

20 Deb Dana, *Polyvagal Theory: Using the Autonomic Ladder to Work with Perfectionism* (Mansfield, CT: The National Institute for the Clinical Application of Behavioral Medicine, 2018).

To say it another way, the middle of the ladder is your sympathetic (arousal) state, and both top and bottom are parasympathetic (rest, non-arousal, or shutdown).

According to this theory, you must go up and down the ladder sequentially, so if you are at the bottom, to get back to the ideal state at the top, you need to traverse the middle, which might lead you through a state of stress, arousal, higher energy, tears, and so forth.[21]

If you want to use PVT when engaging with others, understand your colleague, partner, friend, and so forth will get cues from your nervous system through a process of co-regulation.[22] The best thing you can do is just be there with them and "co-regulate" by coming from a place of ventral vagal (top of ladder) yourself. It is also important to note someone in dorsal vagal (bottom of ladder) can be shut down and therefore behave akin to a turtle inside their shell. In order to help this person, knocking on the shell and demanding they come out will not actually work, and may worsen the situation.

Looking back at *Le Mans*, the screaming really did not help me or the driver regulate our own emotions and sense of control. Though I am sure the driver was used to it in a way, I felt very frozen, and that took away some of the fun of the experience. Though difficult in a race car, I may have been

21   Ibid.

22   Deb Dana, *Polyvagal Theory: Using the Autonomic Ladder to Work with Perfectionism* (Mansfield, CT: The National Institute for the Clinical Application of Behavioral Medicine, 2018).

able to get back to ventral vagal with more breathing meditation and visualization, which I describe later in this book.

POLYVAGAL EXAMPLE

Mike is a senior vice president of technology at a major organization. His job is to make sure his team "puts out the fires" and makes everything run smoothly, even late at night and on holidays. When I met with Mike, he was facing challenging conflicts at work and at home. I introduced him to the polyvagal theory, an instant light bulb went off for him about a recurring pattern in his communication.

"So when I'm avoiding this conversation with a high-conflict peer, I am in my turtle shell, trying to hide," he explained. "When my wife and I argue, and she raises her voice in animation, I immediately slow down, shut down, and get quiet. We now understand her being animated [sympathetic state in the middle of the polyvagal ladder] is her request I engage in the conversation, but I'm already [at the bottom of the ladder] in dorsal vagal and shut down. This leads to continued upset and conflict as we fall into our common patterns."

Armed with this new framework, Mike was able to quickly shift into a more helpful mindset and utilize several of our self-coaching tools to improve these important relationships.

Like it does for Mike (and me), the polyvagal theory can give you a new angle—a new lens by which you can see and improve some of your more challenging interactions.

ADVANCES IN NEUROBIOLOGY SHOW LIMITATIONS

In addition to new research about the role of the vagus nerve, scientists have made tremendous progress in learning about the brain, particularly the hippocampus, the two amygdalae, the basal ganglia, and the prefrontal cortex. These parts of the brain play together to process information, determine how we act on that information, and work to register the information in memory and in the body.

Interestingly, your basal ganglia holds on to your paradigms, mental models, and frameworks that help you to make better decisions.[23] The basal ganglia cannot, however, communicate directly with the language centers of the brain, so it uses your body as an intermediary and interpreter.[24] At times when you "feel it in your gut," it may be this prehistoric part of your brain trying to have a conversation with you, and I hope you don't miss the memo!

For me at *Le Mans*, my gut was telling me this was a dangerous situation but I could trust the person who was taking me out on the adventure. I had context the odds of me being safe were still very high, and that helped keep me in the game and enjoy it, but there was chaos in my brain at the moment regardless. I was sweating, I felt tight, and the adrenaline was through the roof, largely because I could not connect with my gut to get the answers I needed.

---

23 Chade-Meng Tan, *Search Inside Yourself: The Unexpected Path to Achieving Success, Happiness (and World Peace)* (New York: Harper Collins, 2012), 24.

24 *Talks at Google*, "Social Intelligence | Daniel Goleman," November 13, 2017, video, 55:52, cited in Tan, *Search Inside Yourself*, 24.

MIND-BODY RECIPROCAL FEEDBACK

Being human can indeed be confusing, in a good way as well. Here are two tools to keep in mind as we explore self-coaching as a powerful resource for more clarity and success.

There is now a tremendous body of research on the mind-body feedback loop. Yes, your mind can influence your body, but surprisingly, your body can also influence your mind.[25] For example, before a huge meeting, you might decide to "take up some space," change your breathing, or muster up a huge grin. If you have an intention of feeling more calm, relaxed, and happier from these behaviors, you are going to notice an almost immediate difference in how you feel leading up to such events.

Power Posing

The research is very persuasive that our mind listens to our body just as our body listens to our mind. Psychologist Amy Cuddy's breakthrough research on "power posing" is the focus of her TEDx Talk.[26] She advises one to find a safe place where you can pose like a superhero or person of power, and to hold that pose for even two minutes before a major event. This will start to shift your brain chemistry in a positive way. Her advice is based on the beautiful feedback loop between mind and body. This also means if you're in an unhelpful body position or telling yourself to be unhappy, it's quite possible this will translate into actual unhappiness.

---

25 Amy Cuddy, "Your Body Language May Shape Who You Are," filmed June 2012 in Edinburgh, Scotland, TED video, 20:37.
26 Ibid.

Distanced Self-Talk

With respect to self-talk or "inner chatter," if our brain is feeling threatened rather than challenged, this will lead to constricting of blood vessels, increased risk of cardiovascular disease, and the possibility for cellular damage due to inflammation throughout your body, according to new research out of UCLA.[27]

In his book *Chatter*, psychologist Ethan Kross teaches us the value of moving our brains—our inner chatter—from "threat" to "challenge" by using the concept of "distanced self-talk."

When journaling or speaking, using your own name has profound impact. In key moments, this has been noted by leaders such as Malala Yousafzai and LeBron James. When faced with challenging situations—sometimes moments that defined their lives—they both coached themselves by name. When deciding a career move, he has publicly said, "LeBron James is going to do what makes him happy." When reacting to a recent threat on her life by the Taliban, the young activist asked, "What would you do, Malala?" This distancing, it turns out, is a key technique to reducing our stress response, and can literally open up our blood vessels, protecting us from health issues.[28] Moving from inner chatter of words like "I" to "you" or "s/he" can improve mood

---

27   Ethan Kross, *Chatter: The Voice in Our Head and How to Harness It* (New York: Random House, 2021), 41, 80.

28   Lindsey Streamer et al., "Not I but She: The Beneficial Effects of Self-Distancing on Challenge/Thread Cardiovascular Responses," *Journal of Experimental Social Psychology* 70 (2017): 235–41, cited in Kross, *Chatter*, 80.

and decision-making. This distanced self-talk helps to integrate the mind-body feedback loop and help us react better to our environments.

Young Leader Profile: Joe[29] Manages Uncertainty

Joe is an active duty Green Beret (US Army Special Forces) and former professional athlete. He stresses the importance of having clearly-defined goals in the midst of an ambiguous environment. "You want to map out where you want to go, who is doing it already, and then work backward."

He also speaks to the great benefits of having a strong peer group. "It's a lot easier when you have someone right there with you, especially as you are cementing new habits." This concept of "positive peer pressure" helped him during training, when he was first jumping out of airplanes. In terms of VUCA paralysis, he advises you to not worry about getting it 100 percent right. "It is important to be willing to reevaluate your definition of success, as doors open and close, rather than just getting stuck."

The key challenge for readers of this book? According to Joe, the hardest part is to actually implement what you read, which could require you to overcome a range of beliefs that may be limiting you.

---

29   Not his real name.

YOUR TURN

1. Of the concepts above, which resonated with you most strongly? What do you want to do with that information?

2. **Practice.** You can try visualizing tough moments when you reacted poorly or did not perform as well as you would have liked. How was your sympathetic nervous system response? How was the proverbial elephant doing? How might you do even better next time?

3. **Vagus Breathing Exercise.** A brief exercise to help you reclaim calm is to inhale slowly for four seconds, hold the count for three to four seconds if you can, and exhale slowly for four seconds or longer. In my experience, breathing out for just a little longer than you breathe in can be most effective.[30]

"Burdens become light when cheerfully borne."

-OVID

---

30 Christopher Bergland, "Diaphragmatic Breathing Exercises and Your Vagus Nerve," *Psychology Today*, May 16, 2017, cited in Shetty, *Think Like a Monk*, 60.

CHAPTER 3

Embracing "Negative" Emotions (and Moods)

———

"Feel the feelings and drop the story."

-PEMA CHÖDRÖN

Positive psychology—the scientific study of well-being—is all the rage nowadays, and for good reason. Research study after study has taught us a tremendous amount about the causes and consequences of happiness. Our positive emotions are contagious to three degrees of separation, we become happier by journaling "three good things" every night, and money does buy happiness, when we spend it on others. You can even trick your brain to make you happy by holding a smile. All of this is in the research.[31]

---

31 James H. Fowler and Nicholas A. Christakis, "Dynamic Spread of Happiness in a Large Social Network: Longitudinal Analysis over 20 Years in the Framingham Heart Study," *BMJ*, no. 337 (December 2008): a2338 (emotions are contagious); Christopher Peterson, *A Primer in Positive Psychology* (Oxford: Oxford University Press, 2006), 99–100 (three good

Focusing on happiness and well-being does not mean also ignoring the negative. It's like an iconic sailboat—the base ("hull") needs to be there, even as the sails are many times larger than the base. We need some aspect of negative to anchor the optimism.

One element in the field of positive psychology is the (admittedly controversial) Losada ratio, which teaches us that in order to have flourishing relationships, we need to express more positive words and phrases than negative ones. In the workplace, the ideal ratio is three positive words or phrases used to every negative one you introduce (3:1). At home or in your family relationships, the ratio increases to 5:1—that's five positive phrases for every negative one.[32]

For example, written work products generate far more critical feedback and "red-lining" than positive comments. Tech glitches are remembered even though the content is forgotten. We like to catch what's going wrong and harp on weaknesses.

"To change the game, we need to change the frame," as peacemaker William Ury says in his iconic TEDx Talk.[33] If you are

---

things); Christopher Peterson, "Discover the 'other' in yourself," in *The World Book of Happiness*, ed. Leo Bormans (Singapore: Marshall Cavendish, 2011), 18 (money can buy happiness); Nicole Spector, "Smiling Can Trick Your Brain into Happiness — and Boost Your Health," *CNBC News*, November 28, 2017 (smiles can trick your brain).

32 Barbara L. Fredrickson and Marcial F. Losada, "Positive Affect and the Complex Dynamics of Human Flourishing," *American Psychologist* 60, no. 7 (2005): 678–86 (The precise numbers in the ratio raise debate).

33 William Ury, "The Walk from 'No' to 'Yes'," filmed October 2010 in Chicago, IL, TED video, 18:30.

using one positive to three negatives (1:3) today, what would it take to use three positives to one negative (3:1) tomorrow?

It is a little easier than you think.

How does it work? Say you come home and your spouse cleaned the dining room table, researched some new things about finances, and was preparing dinner.

Your options are:

1. Come in and whine about your day.
2. Complain about how your spouse has moved and possibly lost important things on the dining room table.
3. Say hello and talk about any number of other things.
4. (Ideally) thank them for preparing dinner and express some appreciation for the food and their hard work.

You will have other ideas but let's use this list here.

Of course, we always default to option four, right?

No?

Why not?

Because we are not attuned to this idea of "positive coding." In most healthy relationships (including among colleagues and friends), the more positive words and phrases you invest into the relationship, the stronger psychological safety and authenticity you are creating.

A master coach I know was recently coaching an accomplished mental health leader in Australia. When the coachee reflected on the people she admired in response to a coaching question, she described her best friend and began to cry. This friend was genuine, committed, present, and consistent in telling people exactly how much they meant to her at every single encounter. The level of open-heartedness, connection, and mutual respect was palpable in that back-and-forth, and brought the coachee to tears in just recalling it. This speaks to how powerful, authentic, and open-hearted relationships can be when built on a foundation of positivity and mutual respect.

To show up as our best selves for others, we have no choice but to face our demons as well.

The remainder of this chapter explores the three "negative" emotions of anger, fear, and pain, and what to do about them.

The Why of Anger

For many, their Achilles' heel is anger. Anger is a ubiquitous emotion, and thankfully, our response to it is up to us.

As Pema Chödrön explains, "An emotion like anger that's an automatic response lasts just ninety seconds from the moment it's triggered until it runs its course. One and a half minutes, that's all. When it lasts any longer, which it usually does, it's because we've chosen to rekindle it."

To Chödrön's point, there is almost always something stoking the flame of anger. Oftentimes a fear or a pain will present itself as anger. At times, an angry reaction can also teach us a great deal about values that are violated or needs that are unmet. If you can get clear on why you are angry, that is often half the battle, and it can be very instructive.

I wanted to explore the nature of anger, so I started with myself. For me, it began with the realization I was giving up my power and control when I became angry. I also studied the brain and the amygdala hijack, to better understand what it is that is causing the reaction. When thinking about being "poised under pressure," I developed a persona of a Laughing Buddha, or Tigger from *Winnie the Pooh*, to remind me to lighten up. To reinforce the commitment, I remind myself of the lesson from the ancient Tibetan text Lamrim, that the root problem with anger is it inflicts harm on another.[34] My anger can hurt someone else.

It is also important to notice being angry for long periods of time often indicates you may actually be angry at yourself rather than the other person. What did you let them do? Were you complicit? Did you avoid a confrontation, compromise your values, or trust someone when you might have been more careful? I run into this a lot, where clients remain angry for a long time only to realize the anger is directed at themselves.

Acceptance and forgiveness are the dual keys to dissipate anger. These are hard lessons—to find a way to accept and forgive—and yet it is the way to go as you strive to serve yourself.

---

34 Karin Valham, Comp., *Extended Lam-Rim Outlines: Beginners' Meditation Guide* (Kathmandu, Nepal: Kopan Monastery, 2012), 65.

Reflection

As Aristotle said, "Anybody can become angry—that is easy; but to be angry with the right person, and to the right degree, and at the right time, and for the right purpose, and in the right way—that is not within everybody's power and is not easy."

What do you make of this quote and how does it apply in your life?

Methodically Examining Fears

Well before Tim Ferriss became a celebrated author, investor, and podcast host with a net worth exceeding one hundred million dollars, he came very close to dying from the disease of depression on one hopeless day.[35] One day he was happy and the next day he wasn't; how fragile this balance can be.[36]

"I was sitting in the back of my minivan in the campus parking lot, when I decided I was going to commit suicide," he explains. "And I went from deciding to full-blown planning very quickly."[37]

He tells us this harrowing story in his TEDx Talk on fear-setting, which is about stoic philosophy, reflecting on fear, and finding ways to mitigate risk by exploring it from different angles. Ferriss explains he has bipolar disorder and has had

---

35 Timothy Ferriss, "Why you Should Define your Fears Instead of your Goals," filmed April 2017 in Vancouver, BC, TED video, 13:14.

36 If you feel you are in crisis, please call the US National Suicide Prevention Lifeline, a free, 24-hour hotline, at 1.800.273.8255. They can help.

37 Timothy Ferriss, "Why you Should Define your Fears Instead of your Goals," filmed April 2017 in Vancouver, BC, TED video, 13:14.

suicidal ideation before. His bipolarity was a real threat to his well-being, having had over fifty major depressive episodes in his life, so he took steps to address it.

In stoic philosophy, a key learning is to practice "premeditation of fears," which is a fancy way of saying we should sit with the worst-case scenario, understand it, and then find ways to mitigate and repair the risk.[38] Stoics strive to accept life as it is, to honor the good and the bad with equanimity, and to plow forward even when things are not always rosy.

One such process to address and mitigate fear is developed by Ferriss and is called "fear-setting." The premise is quite simple and you can do it right now. Think of something you are afraid of. It can be a big fear or small fear, immediate or far into the future.

Now that you have identified the fear, define the worst-case scenario—what if things really blow up (step one)?

Now we want to look at what can be done to prevent that worse-case scenario from occurring (step two), followed by ways we can repair the situation if the worst-case scenario still happens (step three).

Once you've gotten there, the next two steps are a piece of cake. Next up, you want to explore the benefits of success (even partial success) (step four), and then finally, the consequences of not taking the action you are afraid of (step five).

---

38 "A Stoic Response to Fear," Daily Stoic, accessed February 20, 2021.

In summary, if you are afraid to take a particular action, you can examine:

1. Worst-case scenario as a result of action
2. How to prevent worst-case scenario
3. How to repair worst-case if it happens
4. Benefits if original action is successful (even partially)
5. Consequences of inaction

Let me put it into context for you.

Say hypothetically you are writing a book and are afraid in a worst-case scenario you would spend twenty thousand dollars and countless hours on the book and no one would read it. You can prevent this worst-case scenario from occurring by finding creative ways to invest less and creative ways to publicize more, say through a crowdfunding campaign or other innovative ways to build a readership at the earliest stages.

If somehow the worst-case scenario still occurs, you can repair it by repackaging the book into an online course or blog posts, or using the concepts in a private coaching practice in service of paying clients.

You might realize in doing this exercise, the odds of the book being a total waste are slim, and the benefits of a partial success include personal gratification, a feeling you put something out there that might help even one person, and the natural benefits of being a published author, including some level of publicity and encouragement from external sources.

It also might help you get "over the hump" and allow you to be even more prepared to write a second book.

Now, finally the consequences of inaction are you might miss an opportunity to make a difference and share what you know, and in doing so, you might defer the dream of becoming a published author. If you delay now, maybe you will delay forever, and the excuses will only pile up.

Running through the whole thing and writing it out can take anywhere from five to thirty minutes and can be very powerful.

Young Leader Profile: Jerico Examines His Fears

Jerico Agdan is a Seth Godin Fellow and a prolific young serial entrepreneur living in Spain. In working through his many goals and dreams, Jerico was introduced to the fear-setting concept and was able to use it to his advantage.

Jerico was exploring the possibility of acquiring a license to run a local TEDx event. In engaging the fear-setting method, he was able to solidify his decision to pursue the license. "In a nutshell, it helped me to develop a roadmap with specific steps," he explains. Using the framework helped him realize the potential risk of inaction—that someone else would acquire the coveted license, so he decided to go for it even if he did not feel fully prepared to take it on.

It really is that simple. Examining our fears helps us to look at what might happen if we do not act, what we might lose by acting, and how that balancing act works out, considering many angles. In Jerico's case, it created a level of clarity that allowed him to move forward.

Reflection

1. What is one fear you are holding on to, and how might you revisit it through the fear-setting context?

2. Jay Shetty has a "fear meditation," where he sits with a fear and asks himself periodically what he is really scared about, and then asks again, what is he really scared of, going deeper by several levels.[39] By asking yourself what the source of the fear is, you can check your assumptions and sometimes get to a whole new level of life-changing awareness.

Gently Digging Into the Pain

Have you ever gone to physical therapy for an injury? If you have, you know sometimes those therapeutic massages can really hurt! A good technician will dig in there a little, because to some extent, the pain is an indication of future healing. We need to work the pain, and accept it, in order to really make progress in our range of motion.

Our society tends to ignore or neutralize the pain. We like to complain about the pain without really taking the positive steps to address the root of it. Next time you are inclined to

---

39 Jay Shetty, *Think Like a Monk: Train Your Mind for Peace and Purpose Every Day* (New York: Simon and Schuster, 2020), 46–48.

neglect the pain, whether it be physical, emotional, or spiritual, consider the following:

Felt Sense Prayer

I am the pain in your head, the knot in your stomach, the unspoken grief in your smile.
I am your high blood sugar, your elevated blood pressure, your fear of challenge, your lack of trust.
I am your hot flashes, your cold hands and feet, your agitation and your fatigue.
I am your shortness of breath, your fragile low back, the cramp in your neck, the despair in your sigh.
I am the pressure on your heart, the pain down your arm, your bloated abdomen, your constant hunger.
I am where you hurt, the fear that persists, your sadness of dreams unfulfilled.
I am your symptoms, the causes of your concern, the signs of imbalance, your condition of dis-ease.
You tend to disown me, suppress me, ignore me, inflate me, coddle me, condemn me.
I am not coming forth for myself as I am not separate from all that is you.
I come to garner your attention, to enjoin your embrace so I can reveal my secrets.
I have only your best interests at heart as I seek health and wholeness by simply announcing myself.
You usually want me to go away immediately, to disappear, to sleek back into obscurity.
You mostly are irritated or frightened and many times shocked by my arrival.
From this stance you medicate in order to eradicate me.

*Ignoring me, not exploring me, is your preferred response.
More times than not I am only the most recent notes of a
long symphony, the most evident branches of roots that have
been challenged for seasons.
So I implore you, I am a messenger with good news, as dis-
turbing as I can be at times.
I am wanting to guide you back to those tender places in
yourself, the places where you can hold yourself with compassion and honesty.
If you look beyond my appearance you may find that I am a
voice from your soul.
Calling to you from places deep within that seek your conscious alignment.
I may ask you to alter your diet, get more sleep, exercise
regularly, breathe more consciously.
I might encourage you to see a vaster reality and worry less
about the day to day fluctuations of life.
I may ask you to explore the bonds and the wounds of
your relationships.
I may remind you to be more generous and expansive or to
attend to protecting your heart from insult.
I might have you laugh more, spend more time in nature,
eat when you are hungry and less when pained or bored,
spend time every day, if only for a few minutes, being still.
Wherever I lead you, my hope is that you will realize that
success will not be measured by my eradication, but by the
shift in the internal landscape from which I emerge.
I am your friend, not your enemy. I have no desire to bring
pain and suffering into your life.
I am simply tugging at your sleeve, too long immune to
gentle nudges.*

I desire for you to allow me to speak to you in a way that enlivens your higher instincts for self-care.

My charge is to energize you to listen to me with the sensitive ear and heart of a mother attending to her precious baby.

You are a being so vast, so complex, with amazing capacities for self-regulation and healing.

Let me be one of the harbingers that leads you to the mysterious core of your being where insight and wisdom are naturally available when called upon with a sincere heart.

-AUTHOR UNKNOWN

The point here is sometimes the pain is actually a reminder we need to pay attention to something.

You see, we spend too much time trying to eradicate the pain without really honoring and recognizing its message, and this could be true in any area of life. If something has hurt you, it might need more exploration around the root causes and your true needs in that area. We are animals that follow distinct patterns, so chances are the situation might repeat itself in a different form one day. Wouldn't it be better if you have done the work and are ready to really address it?

In one of my coaching sessions, a man came to see me about a workplace conflict he was having. His community had been ravaged by a recent hurricane and he worked for a disaster relief agency. Things were good, he said, but his manager was being disrespectful and patronizing. Familiar with this kind of situation, I immediately launched into a series of questions to prompt a discussion about the employee's needs, his values, and what he hoped to get out of our conversation together.

We discussed the situation, and picking up on the man's generous and open heart, I asked him if he would be willing to give the manager the benefit of the doubt during this obviously stressful and unnerving time. It was my attempt to "positively reframe" the situation and establish a willingness to find common ground and a way forward. For whatever reason, my line of reasoning struck a nerve and the man just exploded into anger and tears. As I sat there, clearly shocked and surprised (after all, I have had dozens of such conversations and had never gotten this kind of reaction before), I came to learn the man in front of me was living in his car, showering at the YMCA each day, and coming to work with a smile on his face despite substantial destruction to his home and the loss of loved ones in his immediate family. The recent storm had taken a huge personal toll on this man but he was still reporting to work as if everything was normal.

It was then I realized the difficult manager was just the "last straw" and this employee was truly hurting. His commitment to the other survivors and the relief mission kept him fighting each day, but clearly, he had no one to turn to who would actually listen to his suffering during this serious emergency. I sat with him silently as he sobbed, letting his anguish wash over me like a wave. I could only imagine how much he was going through, and I applauded his courage and humanity. I didn't mean to trigger the flood of pain, but it seemed he needed the time and space to finally sit with it. We sat there a long while, talking about deeply personal things, and he finally got up to leave, clearly relieved and with a look of renewed commitment to the work and his team.

This hero left a lasting impression on me, and his journey can be a message for you as well. He was tough and strong, and when it became unbearable, he needed to notice and honor it, and reach out for help.

Reflection
What is your pain telling you, and how have you been responding to it?

Emotional Agility: Applying the Losada Ratio
Sometimes we have to be angry to drive a point across. Sometimes we ought to be afraid in order to protect ourselves. Sometimes we need to be overwhelmed by the pain in order to really ask for the urgent assistance we need. This is not to say we should ignore or minimize, but rather embrace, accept, acknowledge, and honor our negative emotions. Knowing how to pivot with ease is a key skill developed through self-coaching. Remembering to use the 3:1 ratio of positive to negative phrases in our work relationships (or a 5:1 ratio in our home or family relationships) can be a helpful anchoring point. The same ratio helps with self-talk as well.

Making Sense of Moods
Sometimes we are dealing with a mood, which is essentially a cloud or fog that will persist for a longer period of time than just a fleeting emotion. Moods, such as the mood of resignation, can be powerful enemies in any self-coaching journey.

"This is a mood that is very subtle, but it keeps blocking you," explained Alan Sieler, author of *Coaching to the Human Soul*, a four-part series on ontological coaching. "It's a mood that's basically giving up and denying possibility." If you ever find yourself in resignation or another unhelpful mood, just notice it and remember we must also work within the contexts and limitations of these moods when coaching ourselves.

YOUR TURN

1. **Visualization.** What do you know about clouds? There are fluffy clouds, wide clouds, and thunderstorm clouds, among others. Think of your emotions or moods as clouds. What do they look like to you? How can you adjust them and maybe thin out the density, take the edge off, and maybe add in sunshine?

2. **Model.** Plutchik's wheel of emotions is a model that shows the different nuances of emotions. Most people think in terms of a few emotions, whereas there are many. Are you angry or frustrated or vexed or peeved? Getting clearer about the range of possible emotions for yourself and others can be a powerful way to improve emotional intelligence.[40]

3. **Tactic.** Basement to Balcony. When we are triggered, sad, or frustrated, we are "in the basement." What we need to do is to realize we are in the basement and then consciously decide we want to move "to the balcony"—a space above us, which represents a certain detachment

---

40 Plutchik's Wheel of Emotions - Robert Plutchik, "The Nature of Emotions: Human Emotions Have Deep Evolutionary Roots, a Fact That May Explain Their Complexity and Provide Tools for Clinical Practice," *American Scientist* 89, no. 4 (2001): 344–50.

from the situation. When you metaphorically "go to the balcony," and look down at your situation from a fresh perspective, you regain control and reduce your reactiveness. William Ury has a great TEDx Talk on this called "The Walk From No to Yes."[41]

4. **Naming Yourself.** Though going to the balcony or other visual anchors are powerful, sometimes they are too much to recall in the moment. Simply naming yourself (*How should Vik respond to this situation?*) can help to down-regulate emotion at a rapid rate, according to the work of psychologist Ethan Kross.[42]

5. **Support.** Can you look for someone who manages a particular emotion well (e.g., someone who is poised under pressure)? What can you learn from them?

6. **Reflection.** To hone your emotional mastery, you are invited to keep an emotional journal, to include five columns as follows:

I. Emotions experienced and the date.

II. How your emotions influenced the way you observed the situation.

III. Your physiological response at the time.

IV. How your emotions shaped your behavior in that instance.

V. The impact this has had on you as a learner.

---

41 Ury, "Walk from 'No' to 'Yes'."

42 Ethan Kross, *Chatter: The Voice in Our Head and How to Harness It* (New York: Random House, 2021), 75.

(Shared with permission from author and ontological coach Alan Sieler.)[43]

"The process of giving stimuli less threatening meanings can be a very powerful tool for self-regulation, but unfortunately it is not always easy to accomplish. You have to work at it."

-EDWARD DECI, *WHY WE DO WHAT WE DO*

CHAPTER 4

Managing Our Biases

"The eye sees only what the mind is prepared to comprehend."

-ROBERTSON DAVIES, *TEMPEST-TOST*

In the very late hours of February 4, 1999, Amadou Diallo was digesting his meal and enjoying the fresh air as he stood outside his New York City apartment. Diallo had been born in Liberia to a famous trading family from Guinea, and after traveling to many countries, he had settled in New York. He was an entrepreneur who sold household items on the street, and he had been standing outside his own home, without any weapons.[44]

When four plainclothes police officers drove by and doubled back, Diallo grew concerned and motioned to enter his home. He drew his wallet and turned his shoulders to move

---

44 Rafael A. Olmeda and John Marzulli, "Unarmed Amadou Diallo is Killed by Four Police Officers Who Shot at Him 41 Times in 1999," *New York Daily News*, February 3, 2015.

MANAGING OUR BIASES · 79

to safety. Though reports are conflicting, the next few seconds are nonetheless tragic.

A quick motion, a shout of "gun," a flash of bullets, of which nineteen struck Diallo. Shock at what just happened, perhaps remorse. Life oozing out onto the pavement.[45]

Amadou Diallo died just like George Floyd and so many others. Unfairly. Apparently recklessly, or maliciously. Their tragic deaths tell us so much about our society and the growth we must yet endure. They also tell us important information about our nervous systems and how we respond to threats.

MY BIAS CREATES A LENS

When I am speaking to my larger audiences, I usually ask folks to raise their hands if they think they are biased. Sometimes half the attendees in the room will raise their hands, sometimes less. Studies on the "bias blind spot" have shown those who do not raise their hands are likely more biased than those who do.[46]

We have an illusion of objectivity; because we see bias in others, we believe we cannot be biased ourselves.

We all have biases, borne of our contexts, our families, our culture, and historical experience. In some cases, our biases are the product of generational trauma, of stories passed

---

45 *Way Back*, "How We Think Without Thinking: Malcolm Gladwell on Great Decision Makers (2005)," September 12, 2013, video, 1:02:59.

46 Irene Scopelliti et al., "Bias Blind Spot: Structure, Measurement, and Consequences," *Management Science* 61, no. 10 (April 2015): 2468–86.

down, and of words or phrases told to us by those we care most about.

Our job, then, is to notice the implicit biases, to articulate them as explicit biases, and then to stand in opposition to them. Many years ago, I worked with the late Lester Schoene, who began one meeting by saying, "My name is Lester Schoene, and I grew up a racist." Lester was no racist at heart, but he knew his upbringing on a farm in the South at a particular time and with particular privilege created implicit biases he would need to stand in opposition to for his entire life. Lester modeled good behavior by starting from a place of clarity and awareness.

A few years later, *White Fragility* author Robin DiAngelo spoke at a conference I was attending, and I noticed like Lester, she, too, was very direct about her own biases and limitations when it comes to white privilege. Allies have a serious role to play, and oftentimes they do too little too late. Her key point there was we can all always do better; checking in on our own biases allows us to be more effective leaders, coaches, parents, and humans.

MY LENS LIMITS MY PERSPECTIVE

In one study about selective perception, participants are asked to watch a video and count how many times the people in the video are bouncing a basketball.[47] The activity is quick and it requires focus to catch all the balls bouncing. To the surprise of about 50 percent of those watching the video,

---

47 *Daniel Simons*, "The Monkey Business Illusion," April 28, 2010, video, 1:41.

they completely miss the appearance of a man in a gorilla suit who walks across the stage. How could someone miss such an obvious intrusion into the normal plane of vision? Our brains are just that good at selectively perceiving what is important. In this case, we have clear instructions to focus on the balls bouncing, so our brain will filter out the rest. In the Diallo case, that wallet so clearly looked like a gun, and any other signs to the contrary were filtered out.

MY BRAIN CREATES "IN" AND "OUT" GROUPS

In the 1970s, Dr. Mary Rowe was examining discrimination and "micro-inequities" at the Massachusetts Institute of Technology (MIT). "I was expecting to work on big problems like the pension plan and daycare and salary equity and so on. There was a lot of that, but by far the greatest number of concerns that came to me were things that on the surface appeared to be obvious small issues, like a person's name left off of an invite list," she explains to me over the phone.

Mary happened to know Chester Pierce at Harvard University who coined the term "micro-aggression" in the context of racism, so she began a dialogue with him that eventually led to her focus on micro-inequities. "More and more, I was puzzled and interested about the whole series of micro-messages," she explains.

She examined the seemingly innocuous ways by which people establish "in" and "out" groups, e.g., who is invited to a meeting or event, how someone's ideas are publicly received by others, and even how someone communicates a greeting. These issues are akin to death by a million paper cuts.

Mary found we perpetuate micro-inequities borne of our biases, and we would need to address these in a conscious way. "I must have spent…some hundreds of hours trying to figure out, if my bias is unconscious, how can I fix it by conscious thought, and the answer is you can't. But what you can do is to regulate your own behavior in a way that makes the effect of your biases less likely to do damage."

One way to address our bias is to create "micro-affirmations," or ways we can remind ourselves we are all in this together, we are all equal, and everyone is deserving. Micro-affirmations are small ways to affirm other people so they feel included. They offer a way to enhance belonging and reduce differences and divisions in groups, for example, by catching someone doing something right and noticing their diversity in a positive way. Micro-affirmations are an antidote for micro-aggressions or micro-inequities because they are conscious acts that help to rewire your own biases.

"A good micro-affirmation is one that is absolutely genuine and that affirms something good the other person has done. So I now wander through life noticing real achievements by other people. I take note of the good work that other people are doing, and find some way to affirm it. It might just be a smile," Mary says.

Noticing micro-inequities and micro-aggressions is a powerful first step to making a change. Preempting the negative through micro-affirmations is a great antidote for the self-aware leader.

Mary's research is important because it complements more recent brain imaging work around "the Other." Brain imaging studies have shown that if someone is part of our "in" group, then our brains will light up in pain when they are poked by an object in front of us.[48] But if we consider that person to be in the "out" group, our brain may not light up when they are in pain. We do not feel the pain of "the Other" as acutely if at all, and so it becomes even more vitally important for us to be intentional in enlarging the scope of who is within our "in" group.

"OUT" GROUPS THREATEN ME

When a five-million-year-old part of our brain notices a threat, its job is to very quickly act in a "fight-or-flight" mode. At that moment, we are evolutionarily hardwired to stop thinking and start moving. If you've ever said something dumb in a meeting when under pressure or angrily reacted to someone only to regret it immediately, chances are your sympathetic nervous system was actively shutting down your logical brain in favor of an immediate response. This part of our brain—known as the amygdala—is also known as the fear center and does a great job of keeping us out of trouble at lightning fast speed.[49] We've got some big guns in there to make rapid-fire decisions on issues of survival.

---

48   Tania Singer, "Understanding Others: Brain Mechanisms of Theory of Mind and Empathy," In *Neuroeconomics: Decision-Making and the Brain*, ed. Paul W. Glimcher et al. (Maryland Heights, MO: Academic Press, 2008), 251–68.

49   Constantino Méndez-Bértolo et al., "A Fast Pathway for Fear in Human Amygdala," *Nature Neuroscience* 19, no. 8 (2016): 1041–9.

You can probably see how an underlying bias can color our processing to make an "out" group, which then triggers a survival response via the amygdala, leading to a violent and tragic result.

TAKING A STAND

It pains me to think about racism around the world, and it is hard to see what any one person's effort might do to help address pervasive social problems. However, we all have a part to play by checking our own biases and proactively working on ourselves. The first step in countering our biases is awareness, and the next step is action. Then comes a commitment to keep searching for more awareness and taking more action. By honoring and accepting that our brain is built to have inherent biases, by putting one foot in front of the other in opposition to those biases, and by asking for feedback and support, we create the conditions for heightened self-awareness and personal growth.

Young Leader Profile: Divya Takes a Stand

Divya Dewan is part of the incoming cohort at Cambridge Judge Business School, where she will be utilizing her prestigious Forte Fellowship to support the mental health of teen girls worldwide. As Head of Marketing and Communications at Veris, a technology company based in India, Divya has learned first-hand about the tremendous power of allyship.

She writes and regularly mentors leaders around the "Men as Allies" movement, and has been using journaling and incisive self-questioning to explore her own biases as well. "I am reading *The Art of Thinking Clearly,* a book that highlights over a hundred different types of bias, so it is clear to me that unconscious bias is a real problem."

Divya explains sometimes when interviewing new candidates for a job, she has to catch her thoughts. "Sometimes I think, 'Oh, this person reminds me of me when I was younger' and this kind of thought pattern can bias me in favor of a candidate, so I have to be extra careful." But what about other times when that person does not seem so alike after all? "When I am upset at a colleague or a stranger, I try to have as much empathy as possible. For me, it doesn't work to 'put myself in their shoes,' so instead I try to see myself in this other human. I try to remember our common humanity and I try to come from a place of love."

YOUR TURN

1. For an interesting look at your own implicit biases, take the Harvard Implicit Association Test (IAT), available for free online.
2. What else are you doing about your own biases? It might be helpful to journal about your commitment and what you can do as an ally for others.
3. The Search Inside Yourself Leadership Institute has a great micro-affirmation meditation exercise you can try. The idea is to think of other people as if they are sharing the experience "just like me." For example, *Bob wants to have a great morning, just like me. Ali wants to feel*

appreciated at work, just like me. Shaniqua is hoping we make some progress on this project, just like me.[50]

4. To learn more about how our brains filter information, make assumptions, draw conclusions, and adjust our belief systems, please view the TED-Ed video on the Ladder of Inference, called Rethinking Thinking.

"Though we may all be in the same storm,we are not in the same boat."

---

50 Chade-Meng Tan, *Search Inside Yourself: The Unexpected Path to Achieving Success, Happiness (and World Peace)* (New York: Harper Collins, 2012), 169.

PART II

PIECING IT TOGETHER: SELF-CARE

"When we fail to nurture ourselves, our joy is depleted and our capacity to serve diminished. Giving from an empty vessel causes stress, anger, and resentment, seeds that sow disorder and disease. Attempting to meet the demands of the world without first attending to our own needs is an act of self-betrayal that can cause us to lose respect for our value and worth."

-SUSAN L. TAYLOR

When your self-care improves, your ability to self-coach improves and your impact naturally grows.

To get where you want to go, you may need to change your mindset and develop a personal game plan. Serving yourself may take some unlearning and relearning, with a pinch of structure. Are you up for it?

This next section of the book will give you several frameworks and practical elements you need in order to establish a solid foundation for self-care.

CHAPTER 5

Flipping Our Mindset

———

Nothing's impossible I have found,
For when my chin is on the ground,
I pick myself up,
Dust myself off,
Start all over again.

-"PICK YOURSELF UP" -*SWING TIME* (1936 SONG LYRICS)

Life is cumulative, and what we learn in one domain will inherently surface elsewhere if given an opportunity. Those who lament failures or diversions fail to really believe this premise, to their detriment. Part of good self-care is changing the narrative.

FIVE KEY MINDSETS
(AND A QUICK HACK FOR THEM ALL)

These are five major mindset dichotomies that will serve you in your self-coaching journey:

- Growth or Fixed
- Player or Victim
- Abundance or Scarcity
- Contributive or Comparative
- Out of the Box or Inside the Box

The key is the choice you have in viewing the world. After explaining these dichotomies, I will present a basic approach to flip these mindsets at any time. Think of it like "catch and release"—where the first step is to catch yourself in a certain mindset, to notice it is not the one you want, and then to adjust.

GROWTH OR FIXED

Stanford University psychologist Carol Dweck artfully presents research in her book *Mindset* about the fixed and growth mindsets. She explains, "for twenty years, my research has shown that *the view you adopt for yourself* profoundly affects the way you lead your life."[51]

To use a poker metaphor, people with a fixed mindset believe they must play the hand they are dealt and it will not improve. Those with a growth mindset believe the hand they are dealt is a starting point for them to now learn, grow, and advance.

---

51 Dave Newell, "Growth Mindset: The Growth Leadership Series Part 2," *Chidsey Leadership Blog, Davidson College*, May 10, 2018.

While those with a fixed mindset yearn for approval, those with a growth mindset instead have a yearn to learn.

Most people will have a growth mindset in one domain and a fixed mindset in another. Perhaps you think you can grow and develop in one domain, and yet in another you may believe "it is what it is" and you are stuck with what you have. For example, you may assume certain limitations about your artistic skills or language-learning abilities, or perhaps you assume certain capability to grow and develop in these same areas.

Reflection: What are some areas in your life where you show a fixed or growth mindset?

PLAYER OR VICTIM

The next mindset dichotomy is that between player and victim, as Google's former head of executive development Fred Kofman refers to it.[52] Others refer to it as "being at cause" and "being at effect."[53] In other words, are you doing things, or are things being done to you? When we take responsibility and ownership over our part of the situation, we become a "player," and when we let things "be done to us," we are taking on a victim mindset.

Let's explore a hypothetical example. Your first meeting of the day runs over, so like a domino effect, you start to run behind every meeting thereafter. It gets to the point where

---

52 Fred Kofman, *Conscious Business: How to Build Value Through Values* (Boulder, CO: Sounds True, 2006), 33–41.

53 I first heard this phrasing at an Accomplishment Coaching event.

you are rushing across town, stuck in traffic, and arriving fifteen minutes late to see your next client. The usual reaction might be "I am so sorry. The traffic in Dupont Circle was just horrific and my last client kept me long, so I am sorry to keep you waiting." That is the victim mindset, and it creates a litany of excuses. As a player, you could say "I am so sorry. The traffic in Dupont Circe was just horrific and I did not leave early enough to get to you on time. I did not leave early enough because I chose to stay long in my last meeting rather than to cut off my last client. We ran over, and so here I am late to meet you, and I promise it will not happen again."

Ownership makes you a player. Recognizing you have a choice as to what meeting to stay in, which client's time to honor, when to leave for a particular meeting, and so forth all speaks to your control and your ability to have a player mindset. This is a tough example because it's so easy to blame "the traffic," and we do it all the time.

Reflection: In your day-to-day meeting management, do you have the mindset of a victim or a player? How about in other areas of your life?

ABUNDANCE OR SCARCITY

The next mindset choice is abundance or scarcity. Too many people (even very wealthy people) tragically see the world through the lens of scarcity. Not enough money, not enough time, not enough status or achievement, or not enough love or respect. The "not enough" mentality inherently leads to unhappiness and can spur a hamster-wheel race with no destination.

It is important to remember we are enough, and we have enough. As Tony Robbins says, "The issue in life is not about resources, but about resourcefulness."[54] These are more than just words; this is about finding the creativity, the playfulness, and the way forward.

Although she was known for her service to Indian orphans and lepers, Mother Teresa used to run a global operation of hundreds of such facilities, and she ran them with very little surplus in the bank each month. Her philosophy was to just spend what was needed and see what happened next. How? She just prayed on it, and every month, believe it or not, the necessary money arrived for her just in time.[55]

I am not suggesting you throw your hands up and call it a day, but there is something there to think about. What if you truly did believe you had enough? Not just thought it, but **believed** it.

Abundance is a way of looking at the world. If there is enough there, I do not need to stab my colleague in the back to get the promotion. If there is enough out there, I do not need to stress myself into a panic. If there is enough out there, and more than enough, maybe my goals are off, or maybe my habits or my lifestyle are predicated on the wrong things, which are leaving me feeling "less than."

54 Tony Robbins, "Why We Do What We Do," filmed February 2006 in Monterey, CA, TED video, 21:33.

55 Lynne Twist, *The Soul of Money: Transforming Your Relationship with Money and Life* (New York: W. W. Norton & Company, 2017), 103, Kindle.

In this time of tiny homes, virtual Ivy League courses, dollar stores, and consignment shops, and amidst stories of Warren Buffett driving around in an old car and eating McDonald's breakfasts, how much do you really need?

If you are at a stage of not having enough money for basic necessities, trust me, I have seen families who have been there, too, and I understand. There is hope and it takes one step at a time in the right direction. The day you decide to fill your heart with abundance in realistic ways is the day you will be a healthier, happier, and more loving and productive member of your family and community.

Reflection: How does scarcity and abundance show up in your life?

CONTRIBUTIVE OR COMPARATIVE

An important member of my care team is Marsha Sinetar. She has written a range of books, including her bestseller *Do What You Love, the Money Will Follow,* which I happened to pick up at a bookstore over two decades ago when I badly needed it. It was a mini miracle to get in touch with her in 2019 and to start working with her on my professional and personal development.

In writing my book, I found myself reading virtually every other book on the market in the areas of coaching, self-coaching, habits, motivation, interpersonal skills, and several therapeutic modalities. After looking through about eighty books and interviewing dozens of people, I began to compile all my work and present it to Marsha for her input.

What she noticed about me that I missed entirely was my comparative mindset. I wanted my book to have memoir-type elements like Gretchen Rubin's, to have bite-sized learning like Michael Bungay Stanier's, to have exercises and visuals like Vanessa Van Edwards', to be fun and playful like Neil Pasricha's, and other elements I found so good in other writing. Marsha politely reminded me to check in about how I felt when I said this, and I immediately noticed the tightness building up in my chest, and the sweat forming on my brow. *How did she know?*

These authors are fantastic, they are real game changers in the world, and I admire them greatly. But there was zero need for me to be in any kind of comparative mindset with them whatsoever. Why compare when I can contribute?

A contributive mindset enlarges the pie, honors your own voice, and ensures you are coming from a place of wholeness and self-love. Rather than spending the time comparing to others, which causes stress, contribution brings ease and joy. You will feel the difference in your physical and mental well-being.

Reflection: How do the contributive and comparative mindsets show up in your life, and what do you want to do about that?

"OUT OF THE BOX" OR "IN THE BOX"

It is truly beautiful when a simple construct can profoundly change human behavior. Perhaps that is the single most important factor that drew me to my calling for coaching, speaking, and writing. In my work around the world, this particular mindset shift has had profound impact for leaders at all levels.

Many years ago, an elite SWAT unit (that I will not name) was receiving a tremendous amount of negative feedback. These "macho police" were known to bust onto the scene, guns out, make a mess, and grab the bad guy, while leaving bystanders stressed and traumatized. It was certainly not a great reputation for an elite squad.

Enter the Arbinger Institute, which coined our next mindset choice between "in the box" and "out of the box." In their books *Leadership and Self-Deception* and *The Outward Mindset*, we learn when we are "in the box," we are focused on ourselves.[56] We are in "survival mode" and take on a selfishness others notice. People feel objectified and relationships become transactional. *Innocent bystanders, get out of the way, get your heads down, we are taking the bad guys and we are leaving.* That is one way of treating a person like an object—an unfortunate liability as a bystander. Perhaps you have seen it elsewhere when someone skips the pleasantries just to demand a task or ask a question. We all know when we are being treated like an object, and when we are, the person doing the treating is operating from "inside the box."

An "outside the box" mentality requires a commitment to **we** and a strong belief that performance and success are also

---

56   Arbinger Institute, *Leadership and Self-Deception: Getting Out of the Box* (Oakland, CA: Berrett-Koehler Publishers, 2002), passim; Arbinger Institute, *The Outward Mindset: Seeing Beyond Ourselves* (Oakland, CA: Berrett-Koehler Publishers, 2016), passim.

an emotional game. Treating people like people, rather than objects, changes the game in ways no other organizational intervention ever might. For our friends on that particular SWAT team, who were introduced to the Arbinger Institute's work, a simple mindset shift of caring about others allowed them to completely turn themselves around. They quickly shifted to care for the bystanders. One story even leaked of a SWAT member entering a home and going right to the kitchen, to help warm up a baby's bottle so the mother could feel comforted, even as the team did the search and extraction of whomever they were there to capture. Imagine how public perceptions changed![57]

I have worked at and for some of the most prestigious and cause-oriented organizations in the world, but there are far too many people even there who treat other people like objects. You have a choice to treat people like people, by asking about them and their loved ones, giving them space to grieve or manage health issues, stepping in to help with a smile, and otherwise walking the talk of **people first**.

Reflection: At work and in life, do you treat people like people or like objects? How do you know?

FLIP IT

Now that we have covered the five major mindsets for this book, here is the promised antidote. Of course, nothing is easy or as simple as it seems, but the first step in our context is awareness and "labeling." If you can stop to notice an

---

57 Arbinger Institute, *Leadership and Self-Deception*, passim.

unhelpful mindset you have, and name it, the next step is to commit to a shift.

One way to do this is to do a "brain flip."[58] I spoke with global coach and self-coaching advocate Hira Ali, a Pakistani-born immigrant who now resides in the United Kingdom. She told me about her clients' challenges with imposter syndrome and perfectionism. Imposter syndrome appears when we are not sure whether our skills and abilities will live up to the demands placed on us. This can be debilitating because it makes us question our ability to do the task at hand. I have clients with the same challenge, at all levels, so I was very curious to hear about her "brain flip" technique, which she graciously gave me permission to share with you.

The premise is to catch yourself in an unhelpful mindset, label it, and decide right then and there to flip the script, by saying in your head "3-2-1-Flip." Feeling anxious about not getting enough clients? *3-2-1-Flip. Clients came last month and I am doing all the right things, so they will come again at the right time.* Feeling wretched because your manager took the credit or yelled at you in a meeting? *3-2-1-Flip. What can I control, and what ownership and responsibility do I have here? How can I take on a player mindset?*

You get the idea. It may take some practice, but it will likely activate your logic and give you a chance to shift from one

---

58 Hira Ali, *Her Way to the Top: The Glass Ceiling Is Thicker Than It Looks* (London, UK: Panoma Press, 2019), 88, Kindle.

mindset to another.[59] This has worked for me and my clients on many important occasions, and I hope it helps you too.

Young Leader Profile: LeRhonda Remembers Her Purpose

Major LeRhonda Washington is doing her second stint at the Pentagon and serves on the Army Staff operations division as a chemical officer. She will be entering a very competitive PhD program and has excelled by all accounts. When I asked her about how she handles imposter syndrome (a form of scarcity), she described her mental process. "I remind myself that I am meant to be here. That people are counting on me and my mission is to help these people," she explained. She is intuitively tying it back to her purpose, which can be a powerful way to shift mindset in key moments.

It seems imposter syndrome is nearly ubiquitous and may never go away. In a 2021 discussion with the Creator Institute, General David Petraeus, the former leader of the CIA and US forces in Afghanistan, described his own bout with imposter syndrome when he was jumping out of planes and later testifying before Congress. To address this, Petraeus echoes the sentiment of Major Washington—to

---

59   See e.g., Matthew D. Lieberman et al., "Putting Feelings into Words: Affect Labeling Disrupts Amygdala Activity in Response to Affective Stimuli," *Psychological Science* 18, no. 5 (2007): 421–8. (showing that affect labeling drastically reduces amygdala activity).

remember our value and to push past our comfort zone as much as possible so we can grow and thrive.[60]

YOUR TURN

1. **Activity.** You might consider keeping note of these mindsets and how they show up in your life over time. What might you be able to learn from their occurrences that can help you in the future?

2. **Resource.** As ancient wisdom of all faiths teaches us, there is love and purpose to be found in service of others. Using my personal experience, I created the Wheel of Purpose (figure below) to quickly shift our mindset by re-aligning to focus on our purpose. We all want to be happy, and as we gain happiness, we seek understanding, and as we gain understanding, we realize it's all about love, and as we love more, we seek to be in service. As we serve, we become happier, and the wheel goes around and around. What would be on your wheel? You can hang it up as a constant reminder of your purpose.

"Do what you can, with what you've got, where you are."

-SQUIRE BILL WIDENER

---

60   General David Petraeus, "Creator Institute Zoominar" (Zoom webinar, Creator Institute, virtual, December 16, 2020).

THE WHEEL OF PURPOSE©

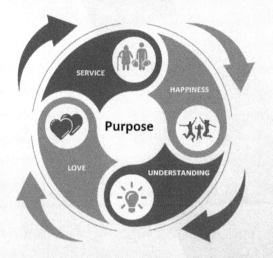

© 2019 Vik Kapoor & Extra-M Coaching and Consulting, LLC

CHAPTER 6

Motivating Ourselves

———

"All human actions have one or more of these seven causes: chance, nature, compulsion, habit, reason, passion, and desire."

-ARISTOTLE

In 2006, my uncle who runs a successful real estate brokerage invited me to a seminar called *Get Motivated!* It was a larger-than-life event for a young professional like me. Continental Airlines Arena, as it was then called, was packed with over 25,000 people, and we heard from speakers like the late Zig Ziglar, former Secretary of State Colin Powell, and pro football player Tiki Barber, among other notable speakers for the times.

I got motivated, as advertised. I try to remember back to that time and what exactly got me motivated. I think maybe it was the energy of the room, and the seeming alignment of our common values. It was also about the vision the speakers created for us, of possibility and hard work, and a commitment to be more than our circumstances.

Ziglar, one of the all-time great speakers and coaches, is known for saying "motivation gets you going, but habit gets you there. Make motivation a habit and you'll get there more quickly and have a lot more fun on the trip."[61]

Over the years, many people have come to me with motivation issues, and I often think of Ziglar. *Make motivation a habit.*

The man was even up there with a water pump, pumping himself some water to make a point. "Do you know what you have to do to make a pump work? You have to prime it! And sometimes you have to keep priming it, and if you stop, all that work you did is lost and you can start all over. The sad truth, of course, is that sometimes you don't know if there's any water in there anyway, and you don't know how deep it is." Ziglar used this pump to prove a point and I had one of those little pumps on my desk for over a decade, to remind me.

SELF-MOTIVATION

Thinking back to *Get Motivated!* helps me to realize some truth behind motivation, as presented for instance by Chade-Meng Tan in *Search Inside Yourself.* Meng talks about the three easy steps to motivation—alignment, envisioning, and resilience.[62] We need to have **alignment** by matching our work with our higher purpose and values, we need to be able

---

61 Colin Powell and Joe Montana, *Get Motivated Workbook* (Tampa, FL: Get Motivated Seminars, 2010), 18.

62 Chade-Meng Tan, *Search Inside Yourself: The Unexpected Path to Achieving Success, Happiness (and World Peace)* (New York: Harper Collins, 2012), 134.

to **conceive and believe in** a better future, and we need to develop the **skills to bounce back** from setbacks.

Though people previously believed motivation is externally generated, the research is clear that **self**-motivation really drives behavior. "…All the work that [we] have done indicates that self-motivation, rather than external motivation, is at the heart of creativity, responsibility, healthy behavior, and lasting change," says global authority on motivation Edward Deci.[63]

According to Indian philosopher Bhaktivinoda Thakura, there are four primary motivations:

1. Fear.
2. Desire.
3. Duty.
4. Love.[64]

Ancient literature from all over the world has variations on this same concept, but what actually gets **you** out of bed every morning?

Is it fear, money, status, power, love, or service? Something else entirely? In self-coaching, we must do our best to avoid self-judgment. It is what it is.

---

63   Edward L. Deci and Richard Flaste, *Why We Do What We Do: Understanding Self-Motivation* (New York: Penguin Books, 1996), 9.

64   Bhaktivonada Thakura, "The Nectarean Instructions of Lord Caitanya," *Hari Kirtan*, June 12, 2010, cited in Jay Shetty, *Think Like a Monk: Train Your Mind for Peace and Purpose Every Day* (New York: Simon and Schuster, 2020), 66–67.

You may also consider particular moments when fear and incentives ("carrots and sticks") were not the motivators, and in those cases, what was? What actually drives you, and how can we use your natural drivers to spark self-motivation?

FINDING "FLOW"

Leading psychologist Daniel Goleman, who popularized the term "emotional intelligence," has called flow "the ultimate motivator."[65] Flow is a concept about peak performance, which is described as "being completely involved in activity for its own sake. The ego falls away. Time flies. Every action, movement, and thought follows inevitably from the previous one, like playing jazz. Your whole being is involved and you're using your skills to the utmost."[66]

When you are in flow, it's because the task is hard enough to be interesting but not too hard as to be overwhelming. You lose track of everything else and find joy in the moment. A good rule of thumb is to try to engage in fifteen minutes of flow per day starting off, and to try and move up the increments when possible. For example, if you know being awake early and journaling gives you a flow state before the noise of the day begins, you can commit to that morning practice.

More mainstream examples of flow include when Michael Jordan "was in the groove" playing basketball, when Beyoncé or Krishna Das are making music, Gordon Ramsay while

---

65 Tan, *Search Inside Yourself*, 135.

66 John Geirland, "Go With The Flow," *Wired*, September 1, 1996 cited in Tan, *Search Inside Yourself*, 135.

cooking, and the meditation of yogis like Sadhguru. Magic happens when we are in flow.

In *Deep Work*, psychologist Cal Newport talks about the connection between flow and deep work. According to Newport, deep work involves "professional activities performed in a state of distraction-free concentration that push your cognitive capabilities to their limit. These efforts create new value, improve your skill, and are hard to replicate."[67] He believes deep work is lacking and will be a prized asset in the future, and it is "an activity well-suited to generate a flow state."[68]

A client of mine who worked at a major technology company would go to the serious effort of moving his whole desktop operation to a quiet room for even two hours, to be away from the din and create more opportunity for flow. I have clients who are new parents who literally carve out their "flow-mos" (flow moments) in the driveway in the car for ten minutes, immediately before or after the frenzy of home life.

Where there's a will, there's a way. Motivation feeds flow and flow feeds motivation. A key will be to drown out the noise and mental clutter that may get in your way of a flow experience.

By concentrating, being still, blocking off time, and setting an intention to engage in deep work, we create conditions necessary to be in flow, and I have personally seen in my

---

67 Cal Newport, *Deep Work: Rules for Focused Success in a Distracted World* (New York: Grand Central Publishing, 2016), 3.
68 Ibid., 85.

work all around the world more flow leads to more happiness, more satisfaction, and more motivation.

You might start to pay attention to your flow states. Is it when you're in a presentation, writing something, biking through the city, or working on your car? Sometimes for me it is when I am (oddly enough) designing a training and arranging the pieces.

VISUALIZING A WIN

Visualizing a positive goal can be a very powerful way to motivate yourself into reaching it. Rather than imagining what you don't want to happen, it can work best to imagine and articulate what you do want to happen. For example, instead of, *I do not want to have trouble with my boss*, the positive reframe would be, *I want to have a positive working relationship with my boss*. This is what is known as an "approach goal," which can provide much more clarity than an "avoidant goal."

WORKING BACKWARD

One way to use visualization is to imagine the end of a project or timeline. If you have a business project with a six-month window until a major milestone, for instance, it might help to imagine the night before the big day. You're arguing in court? Great, what are you doing the night before? And the day before that? And the week before that? And the month before that? Oftentimes working backward can help to jostle new creativity and reignite motivation. This happens because you are giving yourself a positive anchor and your brain is very good at being able to fill in the blanks once you build the vision.

BURNING THE BOATS

The provenance is not clear whether "burning the boats" was a tactic used by Alexander the Great or Hernán Cortés, but the idea nonetheless is to make failure so painful we have no choice but to succeed. Arrive at a foreign land and burn all the boats, so there is no escape. Either we win, or we die. You do not have to be nearly that extreme, but there is value in imagining how this analogy might play out in practice. If you burned the boats and made it very painful to fail on something, what would you have to do? Your creative imagination may come up with some interesting ideas you can use to motivate yourself.

If I need to burn the boats on something, I build in nested punishments. For example, if I need to finish a book chapter today, and I do not finish it, then my punishment is I have to run two miles tonight. If I somehow avoid the two miles, I am required to run two miles every day for the next five days. If I fail to run for the next five days, I am required to donate two hundred dollars to a political cause I **do not support**. My brain recoils at paying the money and running the miles, so the odds of me doing the chapter improve dramatically!

Young Leader Profile: Roman Listens Before He Leaps

Roman I. Kaludi is the founder and CEO of an AR/VR tech start-up he built during his senior year at UC Berkeley. Leading up to his current role, however, was a period of serious self-doubt as Roman struggled to find his footing.

"I had gotten to the point in my college career where I knew my next choices would determine the foundation of my professional life, but I wasn't passionate about the career path I was on. I wasn't truly happy."

"So, I stopped everything, identified what interests I enjoyed no matter how small they seemed, and made it a habit to work on them a little bit each day. Because these were true passions of mine, I found it incredibly easy to motivate myself."

"Eventually, I saw a pattern around entrepreneurship and innovation that focuses on social change, so I decided to launch my own company. Now I work seven days a week with a smile on my face because I have found my passion at this stage in my life."

By making it a daily habit to do things he was passionate about, Roman was able to find the spark to motivate himself over a longer period. Sometimes self-coaching comes down to the small habits we keep with consistency and the inner strength to let the results speak for themselves.

WHAT IF WE FAIL?

Those speakers at *Get Motivated!* had to bounce back from many setbacks. Former Secretary of State Colin Powell got up and told his story of his neighbor, Professor Condoleezza Rice, who he introduced to the US Presidential administration at the time. "Condi" was diligent in her work and rose the ranks quickly. Eventually, as you may know, Powell was asked to step down and Rice was named his successor.

I am paraphrasing Powell because he would have said it more carefully, but the gist of it was, "If you think you've lost something big, think of me. I introduced my neighbor to my boss, and she eventually got my job *and* my private plane!" He got a reaction from the crowd I really enjoyed. Tongue-in-cheek but a tad raw and close to home, Powell nonetheless spoke of his unwavering values to country and friends (he never had any hard feelings about the whole situation). He talked about the event as if it was painful, sure, but it was just one more event in life to explore and overcome.

If he could lose all of that and get back up, find a new vision, and keep going, so, too, can we!

RESILIENCE LESSONS FROM A COACHING LEGEND: PART DEUX

As I discussed in the preface, for this book, I had the chance to speak with Marshall Goldsmith, who is widely regarded as one of the top executive coaches in the world. Marshall has coached many VIPs, including the former CEO of Boeing and the former President of the World Bank while they held those roles.

Marshall and I were talking about one of my setbacks. I was trying to improve myself by using his strategy of asking ourselves questions every day and I was failing at it. I told him I was depleted, he called bullshit, and then I sat there being mopey but recognizing the truth in his words.

I was silent for a minute before admitting he was right. It stung for sure.

We all have setbacks. Sometimes we get into an accident, or we lose a job, or deal with a divorce. Maybe we fail an exam or lose money in the stock market, or otherwise come up short. I've had a few big setbacks in life for sure, and this little failure on my daily metrics was a proxy for bigger failures.

What Marshall did to help me through this setback will unpack a series of best practices that can help you bounce back from any setback as well.

First off, **we got clear about *why* I was having the setback.** Knowing why can be a very powerful antidote for future failures. In this case, the why was fairly straightforward. I could not blame anyone else or my environment because I set my own questions, I knew why they were important, and all I had to do was **try**. If I did not try, I would not pass my own test. My setback was happening because I did not want to take responsibility for failing to try.

So, there's a second point for you. **Taking responsibility for the failure—to the extent you are responsible—makes you a player rather than a victim.** When you are a player, and when you take responsibility (response-ability, or the ability to respond on your terms), then you start to take back control over what you can actually control. That is a very powerful thing when it comes to bouncing back from a setback.

There is my third point, to **focus only on what is in your control.** Ancient stoics Epictetus and Marcus Aurelius said this best—we should not spend any time worrying about things not in our control. Focus on what is in your control, and you can bounce back better.

Next, Marshall said the following: "My name is Marshall. I am cowardly, I am undisciplined, and I need help." He then asked me to take a breath and repeat after him.

"My name is Vik. I am cowardly, I am undisciplined, and I need help."

He did this to prove a point in that sometimes we have to suck it up and ask for help, and to know our limitations. Did your setback happen because you overcommitted on something, or ignored someone's advice? Were you too slow or too quick to act? Sometimes we need to know our limits and we need to know when it's time to ask for help. That is my fourth point—to **find the right help at the right time for the right reasons and in the right way.**

And finally, the biggest gold nugget of them all. My fifth point is about **forgiving yourself and forgiving others**, but primarily about forgiving yourself. You see, when you forgive yourself, you bounce back faster and you prime yourself to "fail forward"—failing in a way that makes it a learning experience for the future.

Voila—a way to help convert setbacks into motivation.

This is how Marshall approached it with me. He asked me to close my eyes while sitting down and take a deep breath. To get into a very relaxed state of flow.

"Now, imagine all the different versions of yourself—all the past Viks (in my case) who had to struggle, and win, and fail, and live, in order for this current Vik to be here right now. Just imagine all those Viks, from the beginning of your life until now, all the versions of yourself who got you to this point now (talking to Marshall Goldsmith). Once you have a strong vision of all those versions of you, gently open your eyes. What do you want to say to all of those versions of yourself?"

My answer was surprisingly immediate. I wanted to say, "Thank you. I love you." And that is the point, he explained. All our prior versions allow us to be here today. We needed those wins, but we also need to accept all the losses too. We need to be grateful we are human and we get to fight again tomorrow. Every time we breathe, we are new and whole again.

I know it's a little esoteric, but the way he framed it really helped me realize the best way to treat ourselves is to just breathe into the new you right now. This version of you is just a tiny bit better than the version of you who was there a second ago, and that's a powerful thought.

To recap, you can absolutely bounce back from any setback, by using the following five steps:

- First, get clear about why you had the setback in the first place.
- Second, own your part of it. Take responsibility to the extent you can.
- Third, focus only on what is in your control.
- Fourth, ask for help when you need it.
- Fifth, accept and forgive yourself (and forgive others).

In my case, I went back to trying those daily questions, and I've been answering them almost every day ever since (with help from my assistant, Philip). My sense of daily focus has gone up tremendously, my sense of balance can now be converted into something measurable, and I have learned a whole lot about what my default modes are. The questions have motivated me to try new things and better live my stated priorities.

A REMINDER IN RESILIENCE FROM MR. REDENBAUGH

Many years after that *Get Motivated!* event, I stumbled upon another talk that has been an inspiration ever since. Look at Russell Redenbaugh. He was growing up during the Space Race, with so much enthusiasm about rocketry. "The model rocket that I was holding exploded in my hand," he explains in his TEDx Talk.[69] Boom. It took his sight and mobility, but did not stop him. Later, Harvard and Stanford Business Schools refused him entry because he was blind, but he nonetheless went to Wharton at the University of Pennsylvania, and graduated with an MBA near the top of his class.

Despite a lot of rejection, Redenbaugh went on to help grow an investment firm into the millions, be appointed to a special commission for the differently abled by the late Senator Bob Dole, and later even became a world champion martial artist, winning the top prize in his age bracket *three years in a row.*

---

69 *TEDx Talks,* "Post-Traumatic Gifted: Moving from Scarcity to Abundance - Russell Redenbaugh at TEDxBend," May 22, 2013, video, 18:00.

How do people like this operate? Redenbaugh made commitments, built structure, and stood firm when the going got tough. At the end of his talk, he cites "Invictus" as a go-to poem for him. Reciting the last stanza out loud gives me some "umph," too, as does *Eye of the Tiger* from the *Rocky* sound track. For some, poetry or scripture or some other lyrical presentation can go a long way to rekindle motivation.

Young Leader Profile: Brendan and Continuous Improvement

Brendan Pilver is President of Lean Six Solutions and an expert at using Lean Six Sigma to improve governmental processes, including for New York City's Department of Environmental Protection and Administration of Childhood Services. When applying Lean Six Sigma to ourselves, Brendan suggests "utilizing the Kata and Kaizen cycle. With Kata, I establish the systems and routines for achieving my goals. With Kaizen, I set specific targets, check if my systems and routines are working, and look for improvements."

Like a scientist testing a hypothesis, you ask whether what you predicted happened. Then you break it apart, asking why it is or isn't working, what obstacles are holding you back, and is there a way to improve your systems and routines to overcome them? You then set targets to test whether your additional improvements work and repeat the cycle. A key is to approach things with a curious mind and view missed targets not as failures, but opportunities for discovery and growth.

"This sounds simple, but it is not easy," he says. "There's a fear to look at yourself."

It can help to view each iteration of the cycle as part of a larger system and apply some self-determination theory in establishing your routines and targets, to give yourself the clear senses of autonomy, mastery, and purpose critical to motivating improvement.

YOUR TURN

1. Notice what activities you engage in regularly and how you feel on the motivation scale. On a scale of one to ten, with one being totally unmotivated and ten being totally motivated, what is your level of motivation for a particular task?

2. What do you want to do with the information from question one?

3. **TEDx Talk.** Post-Traumatic Gifted is Russell Redenbaugh's talk on his resilience, and well-worth a watch.[70]

4. **The Mesh Method.** I bring you this from my colleague Chris Butsch. When in doubt, remember MESH—meditation, exercise, sleep, and hydration.[71] Odds are if you replenish those factors, your motivation will rise again.

5. For a brief, inspiring video of resilience, please see the Nike commercial on YouTube called "You Can't Stop Us." What might be a good, short video to motivate you when you need it?

---

70 Ibid.

71 *TEDx Talks,* "How to Take Better Care of Your Brain Using M.E.S.H. | Chris Butsch | TEDxWaltonHigh," March 27, 2019, video, 17:48.

6. As important as it is to motivate ourselves, we also need to explore whether something just needs to be let go. Maybe the lack of motivation is telling us something, and there is no shame in calculated retreat. See Seth Godin's book *The Dip* for some new perspective on when to quit and when to stick it out.[72]

7. Conversely, sometimes we must burn the boats, like in my example above. How can you do this for something important to you? That said, please consult a professional before making any critical life decisions.

8. You heard about Marshall Goldsmith's daily questions and Brendan's use of Kaizen and Kata. Both systems boil down to making commitments, acting, and then assessing what needs to change. What are some daily commitments you are willing to make? You don't have to have many, but you can start with a couple if you want. I have been seeing tremendous positive improvement with this approach.

"You create meaning when your motivators, abilities, and purpose meet to serve the world."

-TOM RATH

---

72 Seth Godin, *The Dip: A Little Book That Teaches You When to Quit (and When to Stick)* (New York: Portfolio, 2007), passim.

CHAPTER 7

Writing Out Our Needs

———

"A goal without a plan is just a wish."

-ANTOINE DE SAINT-EXUPÉRY

Tony Robbins rushed out of the shower, sopping wet.[73] He flung himself onto the couch and started to write frantically, for what felt like at least an hour and a half. It turns out this was a breakthrough moment for Robbins, star of Netflix special *I Am Not Your Guru* and coach to over three million people via his live and virtual seminars.[74] It was the moment he discovered a new paradigm about human needs.

At age thirty-five, Robbins was already a known quantity around the world. He was coaching elite sports teams, Princess Diana, and other VVIPs. As he traveled the world and met people from all walks of life, something kept bothering

---

73 Tony Robbins, *Personal Power*, read by author (Santa Monica, CA: Guthy-Renker, 1996), audio DVD.

74 Tony Robbins, "Why We Do What We Do," filmed February 2006 in Monterey, CA, TED video, 21:33.

him. It seemed no matter the culture or privilege, people were having the same kinds of issues. How could it be the same issues popped up regardless of place in the world and socioeconomic status? Racking his brain that fateful day, he figured it out, and we're lucky he did.[75]

What he figured out was we all have six primary human needs, and many of them are in direct conflict with one another. For example, we want certainty—the ability to know what to expect—but if you have too much certainty, then you are bored, so we also have a need for uncertainty, or variety. We want significance and to be special—different from the pack—but we also want connection and love, and we sometimes lose genuine connection as we strive for more significance. Those four—certainty, uncertainty, significance, and connection—he calls the needs of the personality. The next two are needs of the spirit—the need for growth ("either grow or die") and the need to contribute beyond ourselves ("the secret to living is giving").[76] Recognizing these needs and their potential conflicts can be very important in your journey of serving yourself. We all have these needs, and each of us has our own internal ordering of their importance.[77]

MASLOW'S HIERARCHY

Before Robbins, we had Abraham Maslow, who created a hierarchy of basic human needs.[78] Maslow's idea is also

---

75 Robbins, *Personal Power.*

76 Robbins, "Why We Do What We Do."

77 Ibid.

78 Abraham Harold Maslow, "A Theory of Human Motivation," *Psychological Review* 50, no. 4 (1943): 370–396.

simple, that it is all well and good to try to give ourselves away and serve others, to offer empathy and love and belonging, and all these grand notions, but none of that would be sustainable unless you first handled the basics. The basics being physiological needs around food, health, sleep, sex, self-care, and so forth, and then physical and emotional safety. Unless you feel safe, secure, fed, and whole, you are not fully able to really grow and have genuine impact on others.

For example, say you are a college student who is exploring what to do with the next stage of your life. You may want to really grow and to give, to support others by donating time to a local charity, and to make a difference in the world. Fantastic goals, of course, but there will be limits and stresses, depending on what needs of yours have already been met. Maybe you cannot afford to volunteer all the time because you need a job to pay your rent. Maybe you worry about the uncertainty of your future because the market feels limiting.

Or you could be a high-powered investment banker, with millions of dollars coming in a year and a global team of traders. You work non-stop and barely see your family, but you provide them with the best resources money can buy. You are an important player in the market and feel really significant, but empty. Why? Maybe you are missing love and connection, or the needs of the spirit (or "self-actualization" in Maslow's terms). Maybe the business of aggressively making more money is not honoring your true needs.

PRIORITIZING NEEDS
The point here is we all have different specifications on these needs, and we prioritize them differently. Some people really

love and cherish certainty, so they watch the same movies over and over again or read the same books or otherwise follow the same patterns. No shame in that if that makes you happy. Some people really need uncertainty, so they do extreme sports or jump off the Matterhorn in a bat suit.[79]

Big issues arise when someone's needs matter more to them than the lives or well-being of others. Many years ago, I observed an MS-13 gang trial in San Francisco. Gang members find their significance through violence. A gun to the head will get noticed, won't it? In MS-13 land, you get a certain tattoo once you've killed someone, and one main person on trial had more such tattoos than I could easily count. In this world, that brought significance, and incidentally a long time in prison.

Another need that goes awry more than it should is that of certainty. We are losing grip on our ability to predict the future or to even have a strong handle on the present. One way to find certainty amidst such uncertain times (i.e., VUCA, post-pandemic, etc.) is to consume television, cigarettes, alcohol, or drugs for example. At least you are fairly sure of how it will feel next, and you seem to regain a sense of control. Of course, this is just ephemeral and can lead to more uncertainty and despair ahead. Again, that self-awareness is key.

Reflection: Of Tony Robbins' needs paradigm, which of those needs resonates most for you, as a driving force behind your actions today? Which of Maslow's basic physiological and

---

79 *Jeb Corliss*, "Grinding the Crack," August 22, 2011, video, 3:29.

safety needs are not always being met for you, and what impact is that having on you (and your loved ones)?

TRANSCENDING OUR NEEDS

Through research by Dr. Scott Kaufman on Maslow's unfinished work, we are seeing an adapted model of needs akin to an image of a sailboat. The base represents Security needs of Safety, Connection, and Self-Esteem, and the "sail" represents Growth needs of Exploration, Love, and Purpose. Interestingly, many people seem to be jumping past or avoiding more basic Security needs in favor of striving for the Growth needs, which creates imbalance and an inverted pyramid of sorts.[80] I feel this sometimes myself, when I am busy serving others (striving for actualization) when what I really need is more connection and a personal break. It is easy to mask intentions if we are not honest with ourselves.

YOUR TWO MOST IMPORTANT PLANS

This section is about two needs-based (or priorities-based) plans you might really enjoy and value. I am not speaking of financial plans, business plans, emergency evacuation plans, or estate plans, but you can find plenty of good resources on those elsewhere. Two plans that are often overlooked are the Life Plan and the Self-Care (or Resilience) Plan, and both are go-to tools in the self-coaching toolkit, for different reasons.

THE LONG VIEW WITH THE LIFE PLAN

Imagine being a futurist. Your job is just to look out there and see what lies in store ten, twenty, and even thirty or more

---

80 Scott Barry Kaufman, *Transcend: The New Science of Self-Actualization* (New York: TarcherPerigee, 2020), XXXV.

years out. I read once that a futurist of a major oil interest had predicted the oil crisis of the 1970s, when the Organization of Arab Petroleum Exporting Countries (OPEC) placed an embargo on any countries that were supporting Israel in the Yom Kippur War.[81] The result was a sudden spike in oil prices (over 300 percent), leading to widespread shortages and panic throughout the United States and its allies. I hope they paid that futurist really well for his insights because his prediction saved the company a massive financial headache.

I invite you to take some time to be a futurist for yourself, by creating your very own mini Life Plan. I learned about the Life Plan from head of Platform University Michael Hyatt and his executive coach, Daniel Harkavy, in their book *Living Forward,* and I have put my own spin on it.[82]

Though Hyatt and Harkavy ask you to block off eight hours to complete a Life Plan in one sitting, I have found many of my high-potential millennial clients love to do the exercises in pieces while continuing to reflect on the big picture. If you are starting to freak out about this idea of a "Life Plan," let me assure you it is easier than you think.

I went through the entire life planning process in *Living Forward* myself in about seven hours in one sitting, and I have seen people do it differently. A rock star client of mine was biking around Mexico (pre-pandemic), and we did a day-long

---

81 Peter Schwartz, *The Art of the Long View* (New York: Currency Double-day, 1996).

82 Michael Hyatt and Daniel Harkavy, *Living Forward: A Proven Plan to Stop Drifting and Get the Life You Want* (Grand Rapids, MI: Baker Books, 2016), passim.

"Life Planning retreat" as he biked from one location to another. Every hour or two, he would send me a piece of what he was thinking, and we would debrief it over WhatsApp before he biked to the next location while pondering a new prompt. It was good fun, and I highly recommend finding ways that make it fun for you. This kind of creativity helps to create connections in different domains where you otherwise would have missed them.

This is what the process looks like.

STEP ONE

- **Core Values Exercise.** What are your top two or three core values? A value is something that goes to the core of who you are and what you stand for. Do you value love, friendship, adventure, status, achievement, or contribution? There is no judgment here, but it is critically important to be honest with yourself. Your plan needs to honor your most important values. If you are struggling with this, think of a high moment in your life when things were going really well and you were on top of the world. What values were present to make that possible? You can also think of a low moment in your life, when things just were not going well. What values were missing there? Hint: Sometimes we forget about how important the values of safety, security, stability, respect, and integrity might play out in our lives, but now is a good time to get them down on paper for yourself.
- **Current Elevator Pitch.** This is easy enough. You can write up four to five bullets that describe who you are so you could explain it to someone in an elevator ride.

- I am Vik and I am a coach, speaker, and trainer with a global practice.
- I have experience running coaching programs for the United Nations, as well as serving as a conflict resolution specialist in the US federal government.
- I leverage my love of learning to serve high-potential young leaders who want to do good and live well in a noisy world.
- I am married and love to travel with my wife (when it's safe to do so).

My example is cursory, but it gives you the gist of what to expect here. Ideally, you can try to weave in your values to assist in the narrative. For now, please do not be concerned about being perfect in your language.

STEP TWO

- **Obituary.** How do you want people to remember you? What would the newspaper say about you? If you can, please take forty-five minutes and write up your obituary, after looking at some examples.
- **Eulogy.** Instead of the obituary, you can just record or write out bullets of what people would say about you at your funeral.
- **Retirement Party Speech.** If the "looking at death" approach is too morbid or close to home for you, imagine you retire well before you die. What do you say in your retirement speech and what do people say about you? Who do you want to thank? What advice do you want to give?

- **Life Priorities.** Let's assume our lives are a collection of our priorities. Do we prioritize health, finances, friends, hobbies, work, relationships, or something else? If we prioritize everything, we prioritize nothing. What are your top priorities? Some people say family, some break up family into parents, loved ones, and kids. Some say career, while others break it up into current career and future career, or side business, or professional development, or whatever it is that makes sense to you. The bottom line is you want to list out all the priorities that matter to you in whatever level of granularity will make sense as we dive into each priority further.

You can use the below wheel to list your priorities and scale them from one to ten, in terms of how much you are prioritizing them right now, with one being not at all and ten being very much so. A good exercise is to also think about what you want the number for each category to be within twelve (or six) months. For example, I might say my travel priority is a one out of ten right now because of the pandemic and all I can do is watch travel shows on television and play pretend. Within twelve months, I hope it will go up to a two or three if the supply chain allows for everyone to be vaccinated by then. This wheel can help you visualize your priorities and how much of a priority they really are for you.

LIFE ASSESSMENT

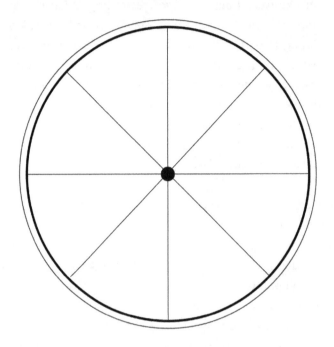

Young Leader Profile: Lorenzo Decides His Priorities

Lorenzo Olvera is the director of the US Senate Diversity Initiative, where he helps to increase diversity, inclusion, and equity among Senate Democratic offices. As a son of immigrants who settled in Idaho, Lorenzo is hyper-focused on his priorities. "My time on Earth is limited—I am a Catholic so I believe life is short, and to me, time is the most precious commodity." How does he want to spend his time here? "For me, that is all about being happy, and that can mean a lot of different things for different people. I'm reminded also of the spiritual side of things. And the love—being in love and having someone love you. It's important to see how these things might impact you. Time is actually way more precious than you think it is. I tell people this wherever I go. You can have all the money in the world, but if you're not healthy or do not have any time, then it's useless." He reminds himself of his priorities by reflecting on his wheel and having a steady flow of conversations with people about life. For Lorenzo, getting clear on his focus and then sharing that message with others has been a great catalyst for his own reflection and self-coaching.

- **Ranking Them**. The hardest part by far is to rank the priorities you created, in order from most to least important. You really do have to be honest with yourself. Once you have your top priorities, which really are the top three? Which can you compromise on and which must absolutely be there? Please play with them until you have a top two. Maybe you can sleep on it, and come back with the answer to the magic question: What is your top priority?
- My Top Priority Is: _____

  _____

- My Second Most Important Priority Is: _____

  _____

- Was this what you expected or did you stumble upon a surprise? Many people find themselves surprised by what they land on.

- **Timeline**. When you look at your top priority, how are you doing on it now and where do you want to be in twelve months? Think of it as a ten-point scale, with one being terrible and ten being excellent. Where do you want to be in five years? How about ten years? You might address the time frames that come naturally to you first and keep moving, because we all think differently on this point. You can always sleep on it and circle back. A decent guess is perfectly fine for the draft. You can repeat the same timeline analysis for your second priority.
- **Repeat**. Repeat the timeline activity for each of your priorities. As you do them, you may be able to start making connections between the different priorities. If a priority seems to conflate with another, you might decide to merge or further distinguish them. If a priority no longer seems to be a priority, or is only a short-term priority, you can label it as such. The key here is iteration and flexibility.
- **Accountability.** How do you stay accountable to your commitments? Without accountability, the Life Plan is just a piece of paper in a drawer somewhere. It is important to find a way to measure yourself against your plan, whether it be through self-reflection or the assistance of a friend, colleague, or loved one who is committed to your success.

That is the crux of it. Easy enough, right? Believe it or not, some people who get super excited hearing about this still never write one, and even those who do write it often find an excuse to lock it in a drawer and forget all about it.

I am hoping you make better use of your time and energy in this area of possibility. You can then keep all these points together in a loose plan and revisit it every year (or every quarter if you are more ambitious). It serves as just a simple way to look at what matters most to you and remember everything you stand for. The long view of your needs.

Young Leader Profile: Jason's Life Plan

In circling back to Jason, who was biking around Mexico doing his Life Plan, this is what he has to say so many years later:

"I'm writing you from Oaxaca, Mexico! The Life Plan and that trip for me has been extremely impactful in my life. At the beginning of 2018, I moved to Mexico and signed up [for coaching] with the intention of getting to the next level of professional, emotional, and spiritual growth, and things were going really well the first couple of months, but it started to become clear in our sessions that I didn't have well-developed long-term goals.

"I wanted to move forward, but it wasn't clear what direction forward was! You suggested this Life Plan exercise and I decided to pair it with an upcoming motorcycle tour vacation through Oaxaca. For me, when I arrive in a new place, it creates a lot of space for new ideas and experiences. Growth for me is easier in a novel environment. So why not, while creating this plan on moving forward in my life, also move forward on my bike at the same time! When starting the exercises, the questions were very new to me and took a while to consider, but once I wrote the answers, they have barely changed after two and a half years.

"It helped me understand the foundations of what I want in my daily life, the pillars that are important to me, which makes decision-making much easier; both micro-choices every day as well as big decisions with major impact. A country's court refers to its constitution for guidance, and my choices connect back to my Life Plan. I use it as my compass, reviewing it every couple months and checking in to see if I am staying true to what I know is important to me, as well to see if the Life Plan still rings true."

Jason is now the Chief Operating Officer of a growing health and wellness brand.

All roads lead to Rome, as they say. But then that Cheshire Cat from *Alice in Wonderland* also reminds us if we don't know where we are going, any road is as good as the next.[83] Plan long and live in the now. That is indeed a tough juggling act to ask of ourselves, but it is essential.

SELF-CARE PLAN OR RESILIENCE MAP

A few years ago, I was in the gorgeous Umbria region of Italy, learning about refugee trauma in an Etruscan palace.[84] Just imagine bold-colored wallpaper, regal park grounds, and

---

83 Lewis Carroll, *Alice's Adventures in Wonderland* (New York: Macmillan, 1920).

84 Harvard Program on Refugee Trauma (website), Harvard School of Public Health, accessed February 22, 2021.

several assortments of the finest foods, along with fantastic company and a very difficult series of topics.

During that two-week experience in Italy I met Charles Figley, founder of the Green Cross Academy of Traumatology and director of the Traumatology Institute at Tulane University.[85]

Charles has been doing incredible work around the US and worldwide, and he has been a great teacher of mine for the past several years. He did a talk for FEMA about self-care and the importance of having a written Self-Care Plan, a lesson I have been sharing for some time now, to anyone who will listen.

Something that can be helpful in the long-term but also very much in the short-term is the written Self-Care Plan (or Resilience Map, however you want to frame it). I boiled my plan down into an infographic that includes sixteen elements from positive psychology and resilience research that was peer-reviewed at Harvard before I presented it at United Nations Headquarters. Since then, people have been hanging up my self-care graphic in psychiatry wards and using the concepts as a quick guide to help people re-stabilize during times of distress.

Others have taken key concepts and made entirely different versions. Some people just write down a few bullet points

---

85 "Charles R. Figley, PhD," Traumatology Institute, accessed February 22, 2021.

of things that constitute good self-care and attach them to the wall.

I encourage you to do anything that visually reminds you of your self-care strategies when you need them most.

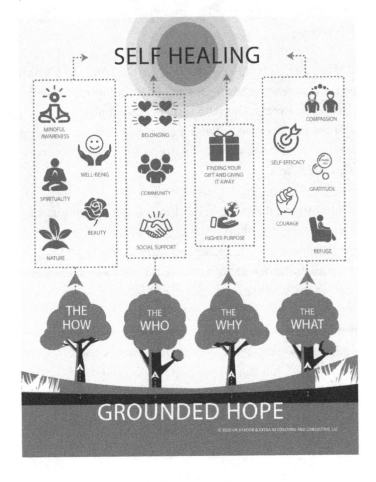

I already know what makes me more resilient. It helps when I chant a bit before bedtime, and meditate in the morning. It also helps when I eat balanced meals, take a walk in nature every day, and spend time connecting with those who make me feel safe and bring me joy. I know this intuitively already, but when a crisis hits—when I really need help—it is very easy to lose track of the very resilience tools we otherwise have at the ready. I bet it is the same for you. You probably already know many things that could help with your self-care and resilience.

This is an invitation to take the time and map out your own resilience plan. You can make a treasure map, an infographic, a vision board, or a simple post-it that you tape to your computer or attach as the background of your cell phone. The idea is to give thought to your self-care and then write down your go-to strategies that can help you. Voila!

As you can see, my self-care graphic includes things like seeking refuge in nature, appreciating beauty, doubling down on my purpose and giving my gifts away, seeking social support, expressing gratitude, and setting aside time for mindfulness, among others.

When I ask groups to build out their own plan, most people can get the whole thing done in less than ten minutes, and I encourage you to try it as well. What we learned in that program for refugee trauma is this builds self-efficacy—the will power and "way power" to get things done—and is far more effective in writing than just in your head.

Charles Figley's Green Cross Academy stands for the premise that self-care is an ethical responsibility, so failure to practice good self-care is akin to professional malpractice.

Please do not commit malpractice—take care of yourself!

WHAT IF I DON'T DO WELL WITH PLANS?

As you likely see from both "plans," they are very loose, flexible, and "living, breathing documents" that will change with the times. They are meant to be snapshots into your own mind (and soul?) so you can stay calibrated. Again, please pick and choose what works best for you and give it a whirl! The best way to see if it works is to try it out.

I KNOW THIS STUFF BUT WHY WRITE IT DOWN?

Another common question I get is around the need to write it down. I am a well-functioning human being, the argument goes, and I know what I need to do, so why bother writing it down? First off, I reiterate what the time commitment is to write it down—it is quite small, and usually less than ten minutes. Even mine, which is a beautiful graphic, just took my designer a matter of a day to create after I fed him the inputs, and nowadays, you have a range of infographic tools online to help you. The challenge you are really facing is the existential reality you might fail, which is made worse because you've written your plans down! It's hard to escape if you wrote the plans yourself and know their importance.

I recently was feeling burnt out during the pandemic, in light of the many calls I was taking with my colleagues all around the world at wonky times of the day. I was absorbing a whole new intensity of stress and despair, and struggling to keep my nervous system in check, which was impacting my mood, my mental acuity, and my ability to enjoy the time with my in-laws and wife.

When I spoke to my therapist-coach about my impending burnout, he nonchalantly asked me about my Self-Care Plan. How's the sleep and refuge? How's the social support and community? How is the spirituality practice and your mindfulness? It took less than five minutes to realize I was functioning less than my best because I had practically thrown my plan out the window at a time when I needed it most.

If you go back and look at Earl Nightingale, Jim Rohn, and many other "greats" in the speaking and coaching industry from decades ago, they all consistently called for us to write things down, plan, scheme, dream, set hairy goals, write them down, and build from there.

They advise we revisit them with hope and with a spirit of endurance. We could learn something from these people, who all went on to be tremendously successful despite uncertain upbringings and difficult financial circumstances.

Writing down things in this way has been shown to improve execution of goals by up to 1.8 times, as opposed to those who do not write it down.[86] This can be attributed to the neurobiology of writing things down, in that our brain elevates the importance of the idea and sends it to the hippocampus for further processing. As you may recall, the hippocampus

86 Mark Murphy, "Neuroscience Explains Why You Need to Write Down Your Goals If You Actually Want to Achieve Them," *Forbes*, April 15, 2018; see also Tom Stafford, "Your Subconscious is Smarter Than You Might Think," *BBC*, February 18, 2015, cited in Hyatt and Harkavy, *Living Forward*, 199; Shlomit Friedman, "Priming Subconscious Goals," in *New Developments in Goal Setting and Task Performance*, eds., Edwin A. Locke and Gary P. Latham (New York: Routledge, 2013), cited in Hyatt and Harkavy, *Living Forward*, 199.

is our center for making meaningful frameworks and our long-term "intuition." Also, by writing things down, you free up working memory to focus on more pressing things, thereby reducing mental clutter you may honestly not even be noticing because it is under the surface.

The best way to see if this has any meaning for you is to, of course, try it out and observe the results! You have very little to lose, and I have personally seen tremendous benefits for dozens and dozens of people. In fact, these plans are being introduced through various courses at top organizations around the world.

A REMINDER ABOUT DESIRE AND DETACHMENT

The *Bhagavad Gita* defines detachment as doing the right thing for its own sake, without worrying about success or failure.[87] In his interview with Tim Ferriss, Naval Ravikant explains the age-old Buddhist teaching that any desire creates pain, because we now suffer until we achieve that desire.[88] He addresses this by limiting himself to a few (ideally just one) major desires at a time, to reduce the pain. When you have too many desires, you may notice stress. That is a sign to revisit and see if you can detach. How can we be active and proactive, without being reactive? By committing to the work and the art, the practice and the mastery, but separating ourselves from the outcome itself. Poker has taught me

---

87 Bhagavad Gita verses 2.4.8 and 12.12. Eknath Easwaran, Trans., *Bhagavad Gita* (Tomales, CA: Nilgiri Press, 2007), 94, 208, cited in Jay Shetty, *Think Like a Monk: Train Your Mind for Peace and Purpose Every Day* (New York: Simon and Schuster, 2020), 164.

88 Tim Ferriss, "Naval Ravikant," June 4, 2020, in *Tools of Titans*, podcast, audio, 16:33.

valuable lessons in detachment. Sometimes you make all the right moves and you put your money in when you're ahead, and ultimately the (random) cards decide your outcome. Detachment is practically a requirement in poker (and life).

YOUR TURN

1. If you like the idea of the Life Plan, please take some time to write yours out. You could do it in one sitting, or break it up into pieces if a one-shot deal is too much to tolerate. Revisiting the plan once complete will allow you to adjust and find synchronicity among the components. For example, I wanted to learn more Hindi and also speak more to my eighty-five-plus-year-old (cancer survivor) grandfather, who happened to be a Hindi professor in India many years ago. Easy enough to couple the two, and it gives him something fun to look forward to!

2. If you like the idea of the Self-Care Plan, please take some time to jot down your own plan and make it yours. What actually makes you feel better? It is important to notice the line between self-care and self-abuse. One Netflix episode may well be self-care, but binge-watching three seasons all night really is not self-care. What actually makes you feel better and helps you strengthen your resilience? That will be the key.

3. You saw my Self-Care Plan in graphic form in this chapter. The premise is to start at the bottom in each area and move your way up, though the path is not linear. What do you like or dislike about this model? What would you add or alter for your own benefit?

"If you deliberately plan on being less than you are capable of being, then I warn you that you'll be deeply unhappy for the rest of your life. You will be evading your own capacities, your own possibilities."

-ABRAHAM MASLOW

PART III

DIGGING IN: SELF-COACHING MASTERY

"For every complex problem, there is a solution that is quick, simple, and wrong."

-DERIVED FROM H.L. MENCKEN[89]

Now that you have laid down the foundation and are clearer about what you need, we enter the realm of deep work. Coaching can be so transformative because it calls upon you to bring your very best to the problems that arise.

---

89 Oratium Messaging Design, Course Handbook at 37 (2017).

The "Power Tools" sections of this book are "Instruments," "Assessments," and "Practices."

The Instruments are objects that can help you coach yourself, and focus on the use of:

1. A Journal
2. A Mirror
3. A Voice or Video Recorder

Related activities that can be done with the Instruments are also provided.

The Assessments are free (or low-cost) resources that can help you to develop deeper self- awareness about a range of personal dimensions. All of them can be completed in a short period of time.

The Practices are meant to go deeper or farther. Please take what will serve you best and adapt from there!

CHAPTER 8

Power Tools for Self-Coaching: Instruments

———

"If you let your learning lead to knowledge, you become a fool. If you let your learning lead to action, you become wealthy."

-JIM ROHN

Jim Rohn did indeed become wealthy, but he was always about more than the money. He had mounds of journals, he stared himself down in the mirror, and he recorded his key learnings often.[90] He understood and used these Instruments of self-coaching, and he never stopped growing.

There are so many others who share this trajectory, and so too can you.

———

90 *Jimrohnfan,* "Jim Rohn - Five Major Pieces to the Life Puzzle Masterclass," June 11, 2020, video, 50:25.

THE JOURNAL

If you journal, you would have that in common with people like Oscar Wilde, Marcus Aurelius, Queen Victoria, Ralph Waldo Emerson, Joan Didion, and Benjamin Franklin, to name just a few.[91] There are many wonderful uses for journals you might also discover.

In this chapter, we will talk about the following journaling practices that may serve you:

1. Gratitude Journal
2. Special Case Journaling
3. Expressive Journaling (Pennebaker Protocol)
4. Morning Pages
5. Evening Pages

GRATITUDE JOURNAL

Research shows keeping a gratitude journal (or simply writing three good things down every night) can help to improve happiness for up to **six months** even after you've stopped doing the practice.[92] The idea is to list the three things you are grateful for and also write down why those things happened. What had to happen for that good thing you are grateful for to happen?

For example, I might write I am grateful for the life I can live, with enough free time and space to read for pleasure

---

91 Ryan Holiday, *Stillness is the Key* (New York: Portfolio/Penguin, 2019), 54.

92 Christopher Peterson, *A Primer in Positive Psychology* (Oxford: Oxford University Press, 2006), 38–39, 99–100.

and write a book for fun. I had to work hard, and I had to have supportive family in order to engage in this pastime.

By explaining the why behind the gratitude, you help to deepen your awareness and prolong the time spent savoring the good. This can be a powerful life hack over time, as you train your mind to look out for what is going well.

SPECIAL CASE JOURNALING

You may also decide to have a learning journal for the key things you take away from each day (a favorite of Jim Rohn's), or a career journal for specific thoughts related to your future career. I personally have a fitness and nutrition journal for my priority area.

When it comes to note-taking, I use "mind mapping" by drawing circles, squares, and lines to help me connect ideas together, because I do not usually go back to read large paragraphs of my own handwriting. It may also help to keep track of any data you are collecting (for example, if you are doing Marshall Goldsmith's daily questions activity).

I also use a journal to map out the pros and cons of a negotiation decision by examining my options. The BATNA is my Best Alternative to a Negotiated Agreement and the WATNA is my Worst Alternative to a Negotiated Agreement—two things to consider when planning any negotiation.

In many ways, writing things out can free up your working memory so you can focus on more important things.[93]

EXPRESSIVE JOURNALING

Yanatha Desouvre's body started shaking as soon as he heard the horrible news of the Haiti Earthquake in 2010. The author, speaker, and faculty member at Miami Dade College is a member of the Haitian diaspora and was deeply concerned.

"My heart is aching and I am trembling," he wrote in his journal at the time.

When his body began to shake, it forced him to write. As he continued to write, in between sobs, he slowly noticed the trembling and shaking in himself subside. The author and screenwriter—no stranger to the power of words—explained the healing power of writing and reflecting. "Sometimes we can treat that paper as if someone is listening to us."

Yanatha has used expressive writing in moments of difficulty throughout his life. For example, he relied on it when his father was rushed to the hospital. Through writing (and sometimes typing on his phone if paper was not around), he discovered the hope and the courage he did not realize he had. "It was something I needed to release. I didn't want him to die. Then I realized that the same blood that runs within him, runs within me, and I began to reflect about the good times we have had together."

---

93   Kitty Klein and Adriel Boals, "Expressive Writing can Increase Working Memory Capacity," *Journal of Experimental Psychology: General* 130, no. 3 (2001): 520–33.

When I spoke with him, Yanatha referenced Mr. Miyagi from *The Karate Kid*. "Balance is more than just karate. It also applies to life." Finding balance and equanimity can be tough at times, particularly in critical or traumatic moments. Expressive journaling can help especially then, just as it helped Yanatha regain his balance so he could support his father's full recovery and help his loved ones in Haiti.

Yanatha's instinct led him to what has now been widely researched—the phenomenon discovered by Professor James Pennebaker known as expressive journaling. The "Pennebaker Protocol" prompts subjects to journal about their emotions in order to improve mental and physical health. Professor Pennebaker found that victims of unwanted sexual advances who told their story, even by journaling, were far healthier later in life than those who kept the events secret. The act of keeping the secret was having an adverse effect on physical health. This idea is also the premise for the Internet sensation PostSecret, where people send in their deep, dark confessions anonymously. Of course, religion has known this for a long time and allows for a range of confessional practices as well. The bottom line here is journaling about negative or traumatic experiences can have a positive impact on your health. Specific instructions of how to use this technique are at the end of this chapter.

Just like we saw play out for Yanatha Desouvre, Professor Pennebaker's theory is journaling allows us to connect words and images in our brain to the appropriate emotion—a pathway that is sometimes blocked by our defense mechanisms. Once the connection is made, the brain can make meaning of the trauma and begin processing it into a narrative you can work with. Absent this connection, the trauma may persist and impact health in serious ways.

In addition to improved mood and reduced stress response, expressive journaling has also shown to enhance immunity, lessen the symptoms of irritable bowel syndrome, reduce pain and arthritis, and improve white blood cell count in cancer patients.[94]

When you think of the potential upside and the actual ask (write about your feelings for a few minutes for a period of a few days), the benefits you receive are far greater than the effort required.

MY EXPERIENCE WITH PENNEBAKER JOURNALING

My late adolescence was a particularly traumatic time for me, as a series of events played out that I later needed to process as an adult. My stepfather passed away suddenly while I was away at a Model United Nations conference in high school, then I changed schools and moved across the country. Almost immediately thereafter, I was in a terrible car accident when I was hit by a drunk driver, totaling my car and leaving me terribly rattled. My mom was also facing immense emotional difficulty at the time in light of her husband's death and left to live in India. I lost touch with her for some time just as I was entering college at UCLA. Together, all these events led to some years of instability, at a time when I should have sought help to process it all.

---

94 James W. Pennebaker and John Frank Evans, *Expressive Writing: Words that Heal* (Washington: Idyll Arbor, 2014), 9–12 (citing a range of studies by Pennebaker *et al* for those who are more curious).

Many years later, when I stumbled upon Pennebaker's expressive journaling, I gave it a try with my then-girlfriend (now wife). We spent time over three days in a row journaling using the prompt. By the end, I could feel a difference. The Pennebaker Protocol is meant to allow you a space to connect with your most difficult, emotional moments. *How did they make you feel? What impact are they still having on you? How might they be showing up in different areas or different relationships in your life?* It allows you to eventually shift the story and create integration and wholeness that can nurture healing.

For me, the journaling started a chain reaction that eventually led me to share my trauma story at United Nations headquarters in New York City—a place special to me because it represented a connection to the beginning of my traumatic chain of events and where I would later proudly serve as an international professional. Along the way, I also quit some bad habits and reoriented my view of myself. This technique has allowed me to process a very difficult time in my life, and I know it can do the same for you.

As you recount traumatic experiences in expressive journaling, I advise using some caution. Once, I was left emotionally wiped out for a day and needed to rest and unplug afterward. Make sure when you use this technique for a deep, difficult topic, you have a solid support structure in place. Seek counsel, plan your time, allow plenty of space, and trust your gut. If you ever feel like you're "going over the edge," please stop. Go have some ice cream or watch a silly movie. Take a breath. There are no bonus points for pushing yourself too far. For some, this activity has completely changed the way they see a problem and its impact on their life.

In 2020, the whole world unfortunately experienced a traumatic year as the COVID-19 pandemic spread and communities everywhere were impacted. Brazil was hit particularly hard, and I coached Guilherme,[95] a UN official in Brazil, at this most difficult time in his life. Guilherme's best friend had contracted COVID-19 and quickly succumbed to the virus. He was distraught and deep in grief when his sister, a nurse, also contracted COVID-19 and had to be hospitalized. Due to the spread of the disease, he was not allowed to visit her as she underwent extensive care in a critical state.

Immediately, I recommended he try Pennebaker expressive journaling to work through his grief and uncertainty. I was confident enough to recommend it to him because I had used it to process my own intense grief. Guilherme said it helped him to feel some control, helped bring him some peace about not being able to visit his sister in the hospital and regain some calm, and gave him the confidence that he could continue to move forward in his life. Guilherme continues to recommend this tool to others who are experiencing similar COVID-19 grief or anxiety.

MORNING PAGES
I was on a Zoom call with Michael Bungay Stanier (or MBS), who is a thought leader in coaching, having sold nearly a million copies of his books *The Coaching Habit* and *The Advice*

---

95 Not his real name.

Trap. Michael borrows his go-to journaling approach from Neil Pasricha's *You Are Awesome*, in which he writes:

1. What will I let go of
2. What am I grateful for
3. What will I focus on[96]

Doing this kind of easy clearing first thing in the morning can serve as positive priming. Other people prefer to just write stream of consciousness for a few minutes in the morning, to clear any mental clutter. Artist Julia Cameron has referred to Morning Pages as "spiritual windshield wipers."[97] Tim Ferriss calls this "the most cost-effective therapy I've ever found."[98] It works because it allows us to unload the messy jumble of thoughts we wake up with, clearing us to focus on what actually matters. My morning practice includes a version of this, tied to my daily intentions for the day, which gives me a hopeful grounding as I get started.

Before I did any morning journaling or meditation, I fought daily battles of doubt, worry, shame, fear, and frustration. I would feel a heavy weight on me when I came out of the shower, over-burdened by my own monkey mind. This went on for many months (or years?) before I started noticing the

---

96 Neil Pasricha, *You Are Awesome: How to Navigate Change, Wrestle with Failure, and Live an Intentional Life* (Toronto, Canada: Simon and Schuster, 2019), 183.

97 Tim Ferriss, "What My Morning Journal Looks Like," *The Tim Ferriss Show*, January 15, 2015.

98 Timothy Ferriss, *Tools of Titans: The Tactics, Routines, and Habits of Billionaires, Icons, and World-class Performers* (New York: Houghton Mifflin Harcourt, 2017), 225.

pattern. Again, it's all about noticing what is serving you and what is not.

EVENING PAGES

It may also help to make some notes about your progress at the end of your work day. Author Daniel Pink checks in with himself for forty-five seconds near the end of the day, to capture the work he completed. Similarly, Winston Churchill was known to say he would try himself by court-martial each night to see if he had been effective that day.

As part of my daily questions practice, I ask myself if I recorded any new learnings from the day. End of day pages can also be very effective near bedtime for those who struggle to sleep, because writing can allow you to offload the thoughts and put them away.

YOUR TURN

1. You can engage in **Pennebaker's expressive journaling** by spending fifteen to twenty minutes a day for three to four days straight. That's all it takes. A typical instruction to yourself might be this:

    a. "For the next four days, I would like you to write your very deepest thoughts and feelings about the most traumatic experience of your entire life, or an extremely important emotional issue that has affected you and your life. In your writing, I'd like you to really let go and explore your deepest emotions and thoughts. You might tie your topic to your relationships with others, including parents, lovers, friends, or relatives; to your past, your present, or your future; or to who you have been, who you would like to be, or who you are now. You may write about the same general issues or experiences on all days of writing or about different topics each day. All of your writing will be completely confidential. Don't worry about spelling, grammar, or sentence structure. The only rule is that once you begin writing, you continue until the time is up."[99]

2. **Positive Future.** One fun and helpful way to use a journal is to engage in a positive visioning activity. You can do this by picking some event that is going to take place in the future and writing about it in a positive way as if it has already happened. You can describe the scene, how it went, how people felt, and what your contribution was.[100]

3. **Powerful Past.** If you feel the imposter syndrome coming or you are nervous before a big event, consider writing out a few snippets from the past when you felt powerful. What were you doing, and what were others doing? What had to happen for that powerful moment? If you can think of one or two powerful moments and write them out, you may notice a shift in your body, breathing, or mood.

THE MIRROR

Dr. Tara Well used to make funny faces at herself every time she walked by the toaster oven in her kitchen. As a child, she was always fascinated by the mirror the surface created and would spend time looking at herself whenever she could. I spoke with the associate professor of psychology at Barnard

---

99 Karen A. Baikie and Kay Wilhelm, "Emotional and Physical Health Benefits of Expressive Writing," *Advances in Psychiatric Treatment* 11, no. 5 (2005): 338–46 (using the instruction from Pennebaker's early studies).

100 Norman Vincent Peale, *Positive Imaging* (New Delhi: Orient Paperbacks, 2006), 19–21.

College of Columbia University, who always knew the mirror could play an important part in one's self-work. She has focused her research on "mirror meditation," which has now caught on at Columbia University.[101]

You might want to use a mirror to help you in the following ways:

1. A quick pep talk before a big meeting or interview. You can also use the "power posing" tool in the mirror at the same time.
2. Self-assessment. Noticing how you feel looking in the mirror at that moment, seeing your face, and analyzing your emotions.
3. Gaining confidence with your presence on video. (For use on Zoom meetings, for example.)
4. Self-compassion and self-love. Getting more connected with yourself through long-term use of mirror reflection.

A mirror works really well to give you a nice jolt of helpful brain chemicals. If you are about to engage in a tough meeting or a big presentation, spending just four minutes in front of the mirror beforehand can drastically improve your sense of control in the event.[102] How? By posing like a superhero in front of the mirror. Amy Cuddy's work on power posing has confirmed the enormous positive benefit of adjusting your body, which then serves as a feedback

---

101 Tara Well, *Mirror Meditation*, 2020.

102 Amy Cuddy, "Your Body Language May Shape Who You Are," filmed June 2012 in Edinburgh, Scotland, TED video, 20:37.

loop to your brain.[103] This can work wonders for developing quick confidence and regaining calm, or energizing yourself in times of need as well.

Professor Well's research speaks to the value of mirror meditation to "break free from stress," "tame the inner critic," and "awaken self-compassion."[104]

I completed her seven-day mirror meditation challenge, which is available on her website.[105] I found it to be easy, and particularly liked you could use a hand mirror, on a table, or a wall mirror you can observe while sitting down. Well's challenge prompts you to contemplate different topics each day, but for starters, you can just make soft eye contact with yourself for ten minutes a day. Just being relaxed and at ease made some of the early awkwardness go away for me, and after a few days of doing this meditation, I also weaved in the information from Louise Hay's *Mirror Work*, which is a twenty-one-day program of meditation, journaling, and talking to yourself in the mirror.[106]

You can laugh, but it is apparently not that easy to constantly say and feel the words, "I love you" every time you see yourself in the mirror. I challenge you to try it. We just forget or we get distracted. We miss these little chances every day to

---

103 Ibid.

104 Tara Well, *Mirror Meditation*, 2020.

105 Ibid.

106 Louise Hay, *Mirror Work: 21 Days to Heal Your Life* (Carlsbad, CA: Hay House, 2016), passim.

love ourselves. That's why one of my daily questions is "did I do my best to love the guy in the mirror?"

The mirror can indeed be a helpful ally for you in your journey of discovery and growth. If you have rather high regard for yourself, a mirror is less helpful to build confidence and self-love, but it can still offer very unique insight on your posture and mood. On days when you are on top of the world or at a low point, a mirror can help you better understand yourself and how the world sees you.

What you may not realize is you have micro-expressions triggered by mirror neurons. This means when you are reading someone else's facial expression, your ability to recognize their expression is tied to your nervous system's ability to mirror their expressions at a micro-level, and vice versa.[107] Working with a mirror allows you to strengthen this circuitry.

IN THE MIRROR, EVERY MORNING
Up until the day before he died, Apple CEO Steve Jobs kept on working. Despite two years of illness associated with pancreatic cancer, Apple simply meant too much to him.

Just six years before his death, Jobs delivered an iconic commencement address at Stanford University. In that address, he said something uniquely powerful about his daily practice with a mirror that offers insight on the end of his life.

---

107 Chade-Meng Tan, *Search Inside Yourself: The Unexpected Path to Achieving Success, Happiness (and World Peace)* (New York: Harper Collins, 2012), 160.

Every morning, he would look himself in the mirror and ask, *"If today were the last day of your life, would you want to be doing what you're doing?"*

On most days when working at Apple, NeXT, and Pixar, Jobs said "Yes" to that morning question in front of a mirror. His philosophy was simple: "If there was a 'No' for too many days in a row, something would have to change."[108]

YOUR TURN

1. When have you used the mirror to your advantage?
2. How might a mirror help improve your self-confidence?
3. If you like the idea of Steve Jobs' mirror practice, please try it out for three to five days to see if it adds any value to your-day-to-day feelings about your work and life. The key is to see if the "No" is present for a period of time. (A general coaching rule of thumb for me is to look out for negative narratives that consistently run for six months or more in a row.)
4. In Tibetan traditions, there is a practice of contemplating your death each morning, and contemplating your life each night. In doing it this way, it inspires you to live your best life that day, and to end the day with gratitude. If you like the idea of this tradition, please try it in front of the mirror for three to five days to see what it does for you.
5. The mirror can also be a powerful tool to evaluate how convincing you are, in advance of an important or difficult conversation. Simply create the script, position yourself in front of a full-length mirror, and notice your

---

108 Minda Zetlin, "Steve Jobs Asked Himself One Question Every Day. You Should Too," *INC*, July 31, 2015.

posture, your facial expressions, and your general presence as you deliver the message. Repetition will allow you to be more convincing for the real deal.

THE VOICE OR VIDEO RECORDER

When time is tight or emotion is high, using a voice or video recorder can be a helpful way to capture certain information and coach yourself. Sometimes listening to your own voice can provide you valuable information if done with curiosity.

Instead of telling yourself, try asking. "How did I feel today? "What did I learn today?" "What was that thing that happened?"

Research has indicated talking to yourself boosts memory and helps with focus. It can also help to solidify key decisions.[109]

Perhaps when you are driving or walking in nature, you are not able to write down what you notice. From what I have seen, younger generations in today's society prefer this voice recorder approach, as they are accustomed to "life-logging"— using tools of social media to videotape or categorize their daily lives for the future. Medical professionals are generally accustomed to dictation of patient notes already and may prefer this audio method as well. With machine learning and

---

109 Jay Shetty, *Think Like a Monk: Train Your Mind for Peace and Purpose Every Day* (New York: Simon & Schuster, Inc, 2020), 157; see also Linda Sapadin, "Talking to Yourself: A Sign of Sanity," *Psych Central*, December 7, 2012.

AI developing at a rapid pace, it will be interesting to see what new technology tools we will have in fifty years.

You can also use the voice or video recorder to evaluate and solidify personal commitments. When you play it back, do you sound and look convincing? Alan Sieler is an ontological coach and author of the four-part series *Coaching to the Human Soul* who regularly uses this practice of voice or video recording key moments with his clients.

"Sometimes you want to ask if someone is willing to make a certain change in their life, and I ask them to go home and record their answers for a few days to see if the tonality sounds authentic to them," he explained to me in our Zoom meeting. "Sometimes if [coaching] is over video, you can also catch meaningful shifts in posture, which open up new possibilities for coaching." This kind of deliberate rehearsal can help clients because it shines a spotlight on limiting narratives or unhelpful moods that might be impeding progress on goals.

Young Leader Profile: Wassila Leverages Technology

Wassila Ould Hamouda-D'Bichi heads the Policy and Liaison Unit for the International Office of Migration (IOM) in Algeria. She began using her phone as a voice recorder in 2016, when she was the coordinator of a program at the International Labour Organization (ILO). While traveling to other countries for official United Nations work, she did not always have the time or space to write everything down. "I used my voice recorder to register my ideas, and then I developed those ideas into presentations or reports," she explains. "Using the voice recorder can allow me to capture memories in any moment, including complicated situations. I also can save my ideas anytime and anywhere, whether at home or in transit." As a mother of two kids and a busy professional with precious little time, Wassila only has positive things to say about using the voice recorder as a tool for more efficiency.

THE SMARTPHONE

In many ways, your smartphone can act as a journal, mirror, and voice or video recorder all-in-one. But is it really ideal to use it for everything? As we struggle with distraction and strive for more deep work and flow, your phone probably does less good than you think unless you configure it a certain way. For example, if you leave it on "airplane mode" and change it to grayscale coloring, then you have effectively made it more useful as a self-coaching tool. You do not want to be getting text messages during your mirror meditations, and notifications about social media and other pings and dings on your phone will only get in the way unless you disable those functions. My advice would be to use your phone sparingly as a self-coaching instrument and instead rely on traditional single-use tools covered above.

YOUR TURN

1. As you think of self-coaching instruments at your disposal, how might a voice recorder or your phone assist you?

2. Are there other apps (e.g., dictation software, efficiency timers, AI-powered reminders) that can help you level up on your self-coaching goals?

"The hardest part is starting. Once you get that out of the way, you'll find the rest of the journey much easier."

-SIMON SINEK

CHAPTER 9

Power Tools for Self-Coaching: Assessments

———

"The act of discovering who we are will force us to accept that we can go further than we think."

-PAULO COELHO

There is a mental model taught in many advanced courses called Johari's Window, which allows us to better assess what we know about a particular situation. I think of it like this: we have four possible quadrants of information—(1) things we know, (2) things we know we do not know, (3) things others know about us we do not know, and (4) things we collectively do not know we do not know.[110]

---

110 Joseph Luft and Harry Ingham, "The Johari Window: A Graphic Model of Interpersonal Awareness" (paper, proceedings of the Western Training Laboratory in Group Development, University of California, Los Angeles, 1955).

In 2016, when describing decision-making about US involvement in the war in Iraq, then Secretary of Defense Donald Rumsfeld was mocked for making statements about America's "unknown unknowns"—but this is exactly what he was talking about.[111] Because what you do not know can prove costly or deadly, leaders I work with are regularly trying to shrink the blind spots.

CLOSING THE GAP

How do we close the gap and learn the things that are unknown? We do this through lived experience, engaging in critical self-reflection, and seeking out constructive feedback. Moreover, assessments unlock a range of our personality traits and patterns we may not otherwise be aware of.

In the field of coaching and psychology, there are many assessments (tests and quizzes) that can give us valuable information about who we are. I do not assert I have tried every assessment out there—I am naturally very curious, but I will never manage to get through them all. The important thing to note is some quizzes you find online are just entertainment, but true assessments are typically backed by science and validated.

What I offer here are a few of the assessments I personally find to be incredibly valuable for myself and my clients.[112]

---

111 *CNN*, "Rumsfeld / Knowns," April 1, 2016, video, 0:26.

112 I get no extra benefit for sharing these with you—in other words, I am not affiliated with any of these brands in any way.

I encourage you to take all assessments with a grain of salt. If you want to learn more about assessments beyond what is here, please also contact a trusted industrial/organizational psychologist or other psychometrics expert. This is not my area of expertise, but you don't need to know the details of creation in order to begin evaluating the accuracy of the results.

Before we go further, another quick reminder that taking the results of your assessments and running them by your MasterMind, your people, your "tribe," will allow you to get more confirmation or contrary opinions about how these aspects show up or are absent in different domains of your life. My clients have very consistently agreed with the results they get, but every so often, we run into a head-scratcher, and those conversations are definitely worth having. In my experience, the combination of assessments and verbal feedback from those close to you is the most effective way in getting clearer on both blind spots and strengths.

MY FOUR GO-TO ASSESSMENTS

YOUR VALUES AND VIRTUES: VIA

Cost: Zero dollars.
Available: Online at VIA Institute Website.
Purpose: To give you a sense of your character strengths, which can be very helpful with big life decisions and career planning.

The VIA, or Virtues in Action, assessment was created by two leaders in the positive psychology movement, Professors Christopher Peterson and Martin Seligman. Peterson insisted it remain free, and it has remained so. Learning about your character strengths can give you a leg up when you align your life to your values.

Personal Example: My result of this assessment lists my top character strength as Love of Learning. Gratitude and Kindness round out my top three. This helps to inform what I need in my life and at work, and the values I stand for in what I do.

YOUR TRIGGERS: SCARF

Cost: Zero dollars.
Available: Online at David Rock's Neuroleadership Institute Website.
Purpose: To give you an idea of which values, when absent, might cause a strong trigger response from you.

David Rock spells out an excellent framework in *Your Brain at Work* which highlights certain factors that can trigger the brain just as if they were survival needs. If your most coveted factors are missing, your nervous system will feel under attack. We are all sensitive to these triggers to varying degrees, and their importance becomes obvious when we encounter situations where a factor is missing.

In times of crisis, such as a global pandemic, knowing your triggers and how to address the triggers of others around you can be a very powerful thing.

SCARF stands for Status, Certainty, Autonomy, Relatedness, and Fairness.[113]

- *Status* means seniority, power and influence, and rank. People may need to feel meaningful and important, and if their status is challenged, this can be a major crisis.
- *Certainty* means control, comfort, and a grasp on expectations and timelines. People need to feel like they have some sense of what is in store for them, what they need to do, and how it will play out. (As you remember from Tony Robbins' basic human needs explained elsewhere in this book, we also need Uncertainty!)
- *Autonomy* is about freedom to act and the skill and range of motion necessary in order to act effectively. It is important to give autonomy where reasonable and to notice if you need more of it.
- *Relatedness* is all about connecting with others, making friends, and building your network of similarly minded people. Everyone needs to feel like they can relate to someone, and that they are part of a group. This is also about discernment between friend and foe.
- *Fairness* is about treating people with respect and parity, so that people are treated similarly. Fairness is a deeply engrained human need and something we are always scanning for in our environments.[114]

---

113 David Rock, "SCARF: A Brain-Based Model for Collaborating with and Influencing Others," *NeuroLeadership Journal* 1, no. 1 (2008): 44–52.

114 See, for example, the Capuchin Monkey experiment if you want to confirm how primates respond when they are not treated fairly. *vladimerk1*, "Capuchin Monkey Fairness Experiment," April 13, 2012, video, 0:57. In the experiment, two monkeys are given a treat when they perform a task (handing the scientist a rock). It starts with both monkeys getting the same treat (a piece of cucumber), followed by one monkey getting

Personal Example: For me, autonomy is the deepest and most important need. If I run across a situation that limits my autonomy, you may well see a reaction from me, but an attack on my status, for example, will not elicit as strong of a reaction. This means a direct report can publicly push back or challenge me to do something without any problem, but the tone and details of the request should ideally leave space for me to act with some measure of autonomy.

SIMPLIFYING HABIT CHANGE: THE FOUR TENDENCIES

Cost: Zero dollars.

Available: Online at Gretchen Rubin's Website.

Purpose: To give you a sense of your tendencies when it comes to internal and external expectations, which in turn helps you create a proper program or regimen for meaningful habit change.

In her book *The Four Tendencies*, writer and thought leader Gretchen Rubin classifies four personality styles based on their relationship to internal and external expectations.

The Upholder can set deadlines and hit them consistently, without fail, because of a certain hardwiring to establish and meet internal and external expectations. The Obliger succeeds when he is required to meet external expectations (e.g., a book club or running buddy). The Questioner can meet internal or external expectations only when she understands

---

a different treat (a grape). When the monkey who receives a cucumber sees it is not getting the same treat as the other monkey with the grape, it rejects the cucumber, throws it back at the scientist, and grows angry, demonstrating how deep the need for fairness goes.

"why" this expectation is important. If it's a dumb expectation, good luck getting the Questioner on board. And finally, the Rebel has trouble with expectations of any kind and follows the narrative of, "You can't tell me what to do because I can't even tell myself what to do." Most people do not need any more information in order to figure out what tendency they are, but if you need help, take the free quiz on her site and you may enjoy the analysis and examples in her book, *The Four Tendencies*.

Importantly, the Tendencies she describes have been validated by medical studies and can be used in the context of healthcare, when physicians are working with patients on rehabilitation and medicine regimens, for instance.[115] In our world of self-coaching, think of the Tendencies as a possible means to explore your own success with any habit change, because your approach would be different depending on your tendencies.

According to Rubin, for each Tendency, one question matters most:

- Upholders ask: "Should I do this?"
- Obligers ask: "Does this matter to anyone else?"
- Questioners ask: "Does this make sense?"
- Rebels ask: "Is this the person I want to be?"[116]

---

115 Jeremy Kirk et al., "Can Treatment Adherence Be Improved by Using Rubin's Four Tendencies Framework to Understand a Patient's Response to Expectations," *Biomedicine Hub* 2, no. 2 (2017): 1–12.

116 Gretchen Rubin, *The Four Tendencies: The Indispensable Personality Profiles That Reveal How to Make Your Life Better (and Other People's Lives Better, Too)* (New York: Harmony Books, 2017), 251.

Rather than tell a Rebel what to do, you are better off giving them information, sharing the consequences of action or inaction, and giving them the choice.[117] To persuade someone also varies by Tendency. For example, Upholders want to know what should be done, Questioners want justifications, Obligers need accountability, and Rebels want freedom to do something their own way. We are more persuasive when we touch on their treasured values: Upholders value self-command and performance, Questioners value justification and purpose, Obligers value teamwork and duty, and Rebels value freedom and self-identity.[118]

Name a habit you want to change. It can be anything, but ideally you want to pick something that has been nagging at you. Overeating? Binge watching TV? Spending too much time glued to your phone? Drinking or smoking? Losing your temper? I know you have a habit you want to change...

What do you think your Tendency is when it comes to external and internal expectations?

Finally, how can you leverage that in service of your habit goals? Knowing this can be a powerful tool in your arsenal of self-coaching.

Personal Example: I have taken Rubin's quiz several times in hopes of a different result, but I am in fact a Rebel. I celebrate

---

117 Ibid., 173.

118 Gretchen Rubin, *The Four Tendencies: The Indispensable Personality Profiles That Reveal How to Make Your Life Better (and Other People's Lives Better, Too)* (New York: Harmony Books, 2017, 229, 230.

this awareness by finding ways to tie things to my identity. I do not sprint because it's good for my health or my doctor told me so—I do it because of my identity as an ultimate frisbee player and I want to feel the wind in my hair.

ASSESSMENT THAT COMES AT A SMALL COST

YOUR SIGNATURE STRENGTHS: CLIFTON STRENGTHSFINDER

Cost as of February 2021: 19.99 dollars.

Available: Online at Gallup's Website, or you can purchase the book *StrengthsFinder 2.0*, or a number of other Gallup books, which come with a StrengthsFinder code.

Purpose: To give you a sense of your signature strengths—what you do best.

For those willing to spend some money, you can gain a lot of important information about your strengths by taking Gallup's StrengthsFinder. Using your top strengths in novel ways can seriously improve your happiness. Also, it is way more fun to work on your strengths and turn them into superpowers than it is to work on your mediocrities and so-called weaknesses.

Personal Example: I once traveled to Omaha, Nebraska, to Gallup Headquarters and its Strengths Summit, where I met wonderful coaches and practitioners who had the full spectrum of strengths. The best part perhaps was that our name tags all prominently displayed our top strengths, making for fun conversation. My top strength is and always has been Learner—I love to learn. Utilizing learning as a primary portion of my work makes me happier and more fulfilled, and I truly treasure learning when I can also share it with others.

Young Leader Profile: Elizabeth & Ikigai

Elizabeth Gamarra has been a Fulbright Scholar, TEDx speaker, and Rotary Peace Fellow. She is currently based in Japan, where she works as the Tokyo Liaison Officer for the Academic Council of the United Nations System. She is also part of the Pacific Forum's Young Leaders program and volunteers her time for the Global Peacebuilding Association and Mediators Beyond Borders. Moving from Utah to Tokyo involved a great deal of change for her. "I invested in self-assessments which Vik kindly suggests in this book (both free and paid), permitting me to tap into my strengths and maximize them in group cohesion with Japanese colleagues. In Japan, there is a very famous word known as *ikigai*. It is the Japanese concept of finding purpose in life, and is a combination of passion, mission, profession, and vocation, but at the center of all these four sub-groups is self-investment. Self-coaching with these assessments has been key to finding my *ikigai*."

Dr. Gordon Mathews has been studying the concept of *ikigai* for over twenty years. The idea, which means "that which makes your life living," is a confluence of the factors seen in the figure below. A note of wisdom from Mathews is perhaps encouraging and informative: Your *ikigai* is heavily custom to you, it will change as you grow, and it is a fundamentally fragile balance that opens the door for a fuller and more "transcendent" life.[119]

---

119 Leo Bormans, ed., *The World Book of Love* (Tielt, Belgium: Lannoo Publishers, 2014), 248.

Ikigai

A Japanese concept meaning
"a reason for being"

A FEW WORDS OF CAUTION

These assessments are just a glimpse into what is possible. Beware making snap judgments and unfair assumptions about yourself and others. We are self-selecting when we answer these questions, so there is substantial room for variation, for example, depending on mood or what scenarios you are thinking about when responding. Do not let any of the results limit you in your life; rather, they are meant to give you a fresh perspective on things and a competitive advantage.

YOUR TURN: PERSONAL MISSION STATEMENT.

Many people ask me what to do once they have completed the VIA and the Gallup StrengthsFinder. One very effective strategy is to create a personal mission statement, which you create using this structure: "I use my top strengths of X to serve a population or cause of Y because of my core value of Z."

Example: "I use my top strength of learning to serve the next generation of leaders because I value giving back by serving and developing others."

You can make any number of personal mission statements, interchanging your top strengths, values, and different causes or populations you might want to serve. Then you might hang them on a wall and stare them down for a while, and use process of elimination to remove some. For many who like this exercise, they have found it effective in quickly being able to narrow a job search. Simply choose not to apply for positions that do not line up with all the variables of your statement! The exercise is equally as effective for entrepreneurs and intrapreneurs who are pivoting.

> *"Those who know both their strengths and their limits become models worth following."*
> -LAO TZU, *TAO TE CHING*

CHAPTER 10

Power Tools for Self-Coaching: Practices

———

"Among all things that fly, the mind is swiftest."
-*RIGVEDA*

Assuming you are not driving, please take a moment now and relax your eyes. Drop into your chair, plant your feet, and take a regular breath in through your nose. You can let the air out of your nose just like you would naturally. One more breath in if you want, just noticing the air as it goes through your nostrils. And now out, just noticing your breathing.

Take twenty more seconds if you are willing. Breathe in and out—in and out without any urgency, just noticing the breath on your nostrils. In and out at a regular pace. And if you get distracted as you are doing it, just notice your distracted thoughts, and come right back to the breath on your nostrils. In and out, again without any rush.

I think the first time I did this, I got distracted within two seconds. Now, on good days I can last several minutes and get back to the breath pretty quickly.

I have done this activity with crowds all over the world, including emergency managers from FEMA and project managers at the United Nations. I tell them what I am about to tell you: "Congratulations, you just meditated." That's all it really takes to refocus yourself and function more effectively. A few seconds of breathing, and you are ready for the next big thing.

Meditation is one of our primary power tools because with very little time and no additional resources, it can help you to both function better *and* feel better. Though I have met many people who admit they do not know how to meditate effectively, I have never met someone who gave up an established meditation practice because it was "a waste of time."

In fact, more than half of the world-class performers interviewed by Tim Ferriss in *Tools of Titans* had some established meditation practice.[120] In summing up his book, *Think Like a Monk*, Jay Shetty also tells his readers, "I can think of no better tool to help you find flexibility and control than meditation."[121]

---

120 *Tim Ferriss*, "Tony Robbins Interview: Part 1 (Full Episode) | The Tim Ferriss Show (Podcast)," October 30, 2015, video, 1:08:30.

121 Jay Shetty, *Think Like a Monk: Train Your Mind for Peace and Purpose Every Day* (New York: Simon & Schuster, Inc, 2020), 276.

In reviewing the ancient spiritual texts, one Stoic researcher hones in on the magic:

The Buddhist word for it was upekkha. The Muslims spoke of aslama. The Hebrews, hishtavut. The second book of the Bhagavad Gita...speaks of samatvam, an 'evenness of mind—a peace that is ever the same.' The Greeks, euthymia and hesychia. The Epicureans, ataraxia. The Christians, aequanimitas. In English: stillness.

-RYAN HOLIDAY[122]

Holiday was expounding on the transcendent state of tranquility that has been coveted for millennia. The innermost calm. He deduced that of all things, stillness is key to a good life.

Meditation (and its lively cousin, visualization) are important practices for that worthy end, and more.

Don't take our word for it. How did the breathing exercise at the beginning of this chapter feel for you?

In all my years of doing it, I have not once heard anyone criticize the time spent breathing, and in fact, it is one of the most powerful and accessible practices in my toolkit. You can't leave home without your breath, so you might as well use it to your advantage. The trick is in the doing.

---

122 Ryan Holiday, *Stillness is the Key* (New York: Portfolio/Penguin, 2019), xv.

WHAT IF MEDITATION DOES NOT WORK?

Being of Indian descent, my "Western" friends readily assume I know a thing or two about meditation, but I assure you this was not always the case. I learned *Pranayama*, or breath yoga, from now-famous Baba Ramdev around 2005 but never really put the easy practices to use. We attended his meditation workshop because a family friend had used the breathing techniques to cure himself from a near-fatal lung disease—a disease the doctors were not hopeful about—so I should have gotten the hint of its benefits even then.

Many years ago, frustrated I was not doing the inner work and therefore not adept enough at the practice to really support my clients in need, I doubled down on my own meditation practice in 2015 by using an app called Headspace. I quickly learned to agree with Blaise Pascal that "all human evil comes from this: a man's being unable to sit still in a room."

If you are a student of modern meditation apps or other video or audio programming, you are aware that guided meditations give the listener direction so they can engage in a targeted meditation for a few minutes or up to an hour. Early on, I meditated for five minutes here or there and thought it was constructive, but I noticed a few things were happening.

First, I was getting very sleepy. Sometimes I would fall asleep even in those few minutes. I learned later that meditation activates your parasympathetic nervous system, so if you are sleep-deprived, it will become obvious. Many clients ask me about this and the answer is very simple—sleep more, and better yet, meditate when you have a high level of natural energy (not bolstered by caffeine or adrenaline).

Second, I was getting very distracted, sometimes for almost the entire period. A few times, whatever thought I was focused on would continue on well after the timer went off. Sometimes, I would notice the thought and decide the thought was more important than the meditation! This early stubbornness on my part was a key indication that continuing to "learn meditation" in this self-guided manner was going to have diminishing returns for me.

I had to make a bigger commitment to myself, so I did. Ever run a marathon without really training? I'm not that foolhardy when it comes to running, but I suppose I can be headstrong in other areas.

THE RETREAT

I should start by saying there are essentially three tiers of meditators. First is the casual one, who has meditated less than one hundred hours total, maybe a few minutes a day off and on. Most of us will strive to be in this category.

Then there is the long-term meditator, who has engaged in 1,000 to 10,000 hours of deliberate practice, which is often achieved through immersive retreats. Finally are the Olympians (or *yogis*), many from the Tibetan and ancient Indian lineages, who literally go on three-year meditation wanderings or who live in austere conditions in near-constant meditation.[123]

To be a better casual meditator, I enrolled in a *Vipassana* retreat, which draws on practices from ancient India and what is now Myanmar. These immersive retreats happen all over the world and are generally free of charge (to my knowledge). You simply apply and attend, and are given food and lodging for your time there. The idea is to simulate the monastic life for a few days, so you can return to the world with new awareness. While at a retreat, you are given ample time and space to reflect, meditate, chant, wander the grounds, and sleep in peace.

There are a few curveballs to note:

1. For new students, the retreat is **ten days long**, no exceptions. Once you are an old student, you can go to weekend retreats.

2. With very few exceptions, the rules of the retreat dictate there will be "noble silence" for the duration, which means **no talking with anyone,** no phones, no real eye contact (keep your gaze down), and no charades or motioning. Essentially, you are there with hundreds of people but you are not communicating with one another (again, with exceptions for emergency).

---

123 See Daniel Goleman and Richard J. Davidson. *Altered Traits: Science Reveals How Meditation Changes Your Mind, Brain, and Body* (New York: Avery, 2017), 248–50.

3. Upon arrival, you will turn over your phone, computer, notebooks, books, and any other forms of entertainment, to be placed in a secure location until the retreat is over.
4. Breakfast will be early and simple. Dinner will be early and consist only of tea and fruit. Again, there is no talking even during meals.
5. You may leave the retreat any time if you are not happy, and you may speak to the professor for up to five minutes a day if you have a question.

This retreat was a rite of passage for me, I tell you. And it worked. I walked away with completely new skills and a greater sense of purpose, but it was pretty hellish every day. People left in despair (a common occurrence at these retreats), and I had several heart-to-hearts with the professor that convinced me to stay.

I laughed, I cried. I secretly cursed my roommate for sneezing on me, and then felt bad about it. I contemplated life and death and love and joy, and discovered new things that are now very much a part of me so many years later. Things like the great triangle of suffering—craving, clinging, and aversion. We crave things, we cling to them, or we push them away. The alternative is equanimity and stillness; a compassionate stillness to let the itch go away on its own without needing to scratch it.

At the end of day one, the professor called me up to the front to scold me for falling asleep in the session. How he saw me in a packed, darkly lit room was beyond me, but I was on notice. To do the required hour of meditation at a time (several times a day), I learned to nap before and after each session. My body was sleep-deprived after my years of neglect, so I needed some serious recharging, and regular napping was the only way.

There was also that pesky problem of the proverbial "monkey mind." Our mind is constantly on the move, as you know, and for the average person, it is very difficult to calm it because distractions and worries abound. Author Jay Shetty shares a great comparison from ancient Indian folklore—"the mind is compared to a drunken monkey that's been bitten by a scorpion and haunted by a ghost."[124] Imagine that pain, confusion, agitation, and fear—the range of emotions we no doubt experience from hour to hour or minute to minute if we let our mind roam free.

Eventually, I came to an epiphany after several days of distracted thoughts and worries and hopes and dreams, but no way to record the thoughts on paper—I was bound to forget the vast majority of any thoughts or insights from these ten days. This was a reminder of the freedom I had—the freedom to stop thinking useless thoughts and instead come back to my ever-present breath and body. We often go from one worry or idea to another in a flash, without realizing the flurry of activity does not serve us.

Despite all I learned, I do not wish this kind of retreat upon anyone who is unwilling. Do not go as a prisoner or out of

---

124 Narayana, *The Hitopadesa*, trans. A. N. D. Haksar (New York: Penguin Classics, 2007). A book of ancient Indian fables, cited in Shetty, *Think Like a Monk*, 146.

desperation, but if you feel compelled to deepen your practice, there is no better way to do it than an immersive retreat.

MEDITATION CAN CHANGE YOUR BRAIN

Many casual meditators are doing the work because they want calm, focus, and ease. These benefits are about a change in state. Drop onto the mat when you're angry and you will likely leave feeling better. Such is the basic and obvious power of meditation. For most casual meditators who sit for a few minutes to an hour a day, this is the Holy Grail of meditation, the proverbial "reset" for your well-being. You can immediately see the ability to react better, to be kinder, to manage stress more effectively, and to enjoy life more. People do genuinely see noticeable spikes in happiness, meaning, and connection through even a few minutes of meditation on a semi-regular basis. Many notice suddenly enjoying an extra split second of pause before reacting in key moments, which can make all the difference.

Studies continue to show promising state and trait changes as a result of meditation—changes in both the current state of mind of the meditator, as well as long-term changes in the personality traits and neurobiology of the meditator.

Amazingly, research can now show you the type of brain waves that are being emitted by people during different activities. One monk emits Gamma rays in record ways (including while sleeping, while the rest of us only emit them during "Eureka" moments). Another monk's amygdala has shrunk over time. Both of them can summon compassion on command, with such strength their brain scans explode in white light. These monks can rapidly shift from a neutral mindset to a state of heightened compassion, without any preparation, which gives them incredible control over their stress response.[125]

We cannot all be marathon meditators, because we have other things to do and dreams to pursue. Take solace in knowing there are plenty of good health benefits of meditation for the casual meditator. These include reduced anger and anxiety, better blood pressure, more focus and concentration, successful evacuation from an underwater Thai cave, and any number of other benefits that help restore equilibrium.

MEDITATION CAN SAVE YOUR LIFE

Ah yes, the cave. The Tham Luang cave system in Thailand is one of the most expansive in the world. When the rainy season arrives and the water level rises, this system has large segments that become unreachable when submerged.

In 2018, the hero of our story, Ekapol Chanthawong, found himself trapped in this underwater cave system while responsible for several boys on the junior football (soccer) team he was coaching. These explorers were running out of air, had no remaining food, and were struggling to get water, and yet they were able to survive in that cave for as long as eighteen days through the use of meditation. Chanthawong was a former Buddhist monk (he is now fully ordained) and was able to build an environment of calm and meditation in the cave for all those stranded. Miraculously, they all survived.[126]

---

125 Goleman and Davidson. *Altered Traits*, 250, 263, 273–74.
126 Zameena Mejia, "A Stanford Expert Explains How Meditation Helped the Thai Boys Survive," *CNBC*, July 10, 2018.

NOTHING TO SNOOZE AT

Some of this can be hard to grasp, but the benefits will start to become clear to you in obvious ways. Noticing your breath, stopping for a moment of stillness, staring out of the window, and emptying your mind are easy ways to recalibrate during stressful times. For me, meditation is like a Swiss Army tool for the brain because it can do so many different things. For example, some time ago I had to pull an all-nighter for a huge deadline at work. Heading into the office for my big meeting, having not slept at all, I took an Uber and managed to meditate in the backseat during the twenty-minute ride. I simply did some basic breathing and then a body scan, to notice how I was feeling in my body in a detached way. This slowed my mind down and allowed me to regroup for the meeting. I arrived refreshed, and it felt like I had taken a power nap of two hours or more! Being able to flip the switch and meditate on command has been a powerful tool for me and I hope it will be powerful for you too.

Young Leader Profile: Chris Deepens and Broadens His Practice

Chris Bonnaig is a graduate of Georgetown Law School and a Board member of the Give Back Yoga Foundation. He is an incoming judicial law clerk and teaches a yoga, mindfulness, and leadership workshop through a program he created called Peaceful Champion.

Chris sat down with me to discuss *Vipassana* meditation, which he has practiced for six years. Vipassana involves three types of exercises: *anapana*, body scan, and *metta* (loving-kindness meditation). Because the latter two are better learned at a ten-day *Vipassana* retreat, Chris suggests people begin with the first one. *Anapana* involves sitting still, closing your eyes, and noticing your breath as it goes in your nostril and out of your nostril. When your mind wanders, do not get agitated or discouraged, just start again. Equanimity is the key to benefiting from this practice. Chris stresses though this meditation technique is very helpful as a daily practice to remain calm and react better to pressure, it is not enough by itself.

"I am more interested in what happens even before the meditation. How are you living in each moment? Are you standing for your principles, and are you being kind and compassionate toward others?" Chris reminds us meditation can help us lead fuller and happier lives, by creating a way of being, and will open more space for us than we think is possible.

WHEN TO PRACTICE MINDFULNESS INSTEAD OF SITTING MEDITATION

Some people just do not want to sit in one place for several minutes. They do not like the process of being silent and still and meditating in a formal way. That is perfectly fine, too, and if you're one of those people, you might really benefit more from **mindfulness** in your daily life.[127] For example, next time you take a walk, do the dishes, eat breakfast, or

---

127 Mindfulness is at the heart of meditation, see e.g., Jon Kabat-Zinn, *Wherever You Go, There You Are: Mindfulness Meditation for Everyday Life* (London: Piatkus, 1994), 4.

play video games, you can get more focused about it. *What does it feel like to have the sponge or controller in my hands? How is my breathing or posture as I dig into the task? What does the ground feel like beneath my feet? What thoughts am I having as my roommate is speaking?* Getting hyper-vigilant about these details can allow us to stay more mindful and present in our everyday tasks, which also does wonders to train the brain.

TONY ROBBINS' MORNING PRIMING

Tony Robbins, who I mentioned earlier, is a high-energy speaker, author, and "behavioral strategist." He was a coach before coaching was really a thing. Though he is immersed in the field and knows full-well the value of meditation, he admits it just does not work for him because he is too mentally active for total stillness. Instead, Robbins has a priming practice anyone can adopt.[128] He plunges into a cold water pool to wake his nervous system up, does some breath work, and then starts a practice which some may consider akin to meditation.

He takes time to first express gratitude for three things. Then he takes a few moments to sit in prayer and connect with his spiritual side. Finally, he takes time to channel that gratitude and that prayer toward his three biggest goals for the day and beyond—his "three to thrive." For this last one, he imagines his goals as already being accomplished, and channels the

---

128 Timothy Ferriss, *Tools of Titans: The Tactics, Routines, and Habits of Billionaires, Icons, and World-class Performers* (New York: Houghton Mifflin Harcourt, 2017), 213–14.

emotion so he can really **feel** the results he expects.[129] He does this mental exercise in stillness, with light music, and it helps him to get in the right mindset to start his morning. Maybe, like Robbins, you just do not find joy in doing "nothing," and if so, you have options. The key is to iterate and see what is actually helping you.

CREATIVE VISUALIZATION AND ANCHORING

Imagine being, doing, and having anything you want. The idea of creative visualization is to just sit with the image you want and soak it in. You want a mansion? Imagine decorating it. Imagine driving up to your home, entering it, and sitting on your couch. Imagine giving money away to those in need. The act of imagining or daydreaming about something positive activates the brain, opens you up to new possibilities, and allows for change to occur. Even Oprah Winfrey attests to the powerful role creative visualization has had in her life.[130]

If you find meditation to be challenging, then why not engage in daydreaming? You probably did it a lot more as a child, but at some point, your brain decided the time was better spent on productive **action.** Maybe it is high time to reclaim this childhood pastime and leverage it in service of your happiness and fulfillment.

Once you have a positive vision, you can "anchor" it with a visual or object. For example, I can imagine myself sitting in

---

129 Ibid.

130 Shakti Gawain, *Creative Visualization: Use the Power of Your Imagination to Create What You Want in Your Life* (Novato, CA: Nataraj Publishing, 2002), front cover.

the *Vipassana* meditation hall with my chair, and this gives me a sense of calm. As I alluded to in an earlier chapter, I also use the visual anchor of Tigger from *Winnie the Pooh*, because it reminds me of playfulness and joy during tense times. Sometimes a special landscape or seascape, an old souvenir, or a lucky pen can help to anchor and ground you, particularly when your nervous system is in an activated state.

Young Leader Profile: Jack Goes to the Balcony

Jack Lindsay is an incoming PhD candidate in Bioengineering at Harvard University and a former member of Facebook Reality Labs. For over a year, Jack had been diligently trying out a range of the self-coaching techniques presented in this book. When we sat down to identify the major shifts in his mindset that led to his success, Jack was, of course, thoughtful. He drew on lessons from the Arbinger Institute and the Outward Mindset to relate better with people. He explored values and needs, and negotiated differently with peers as a result. Jack attributes his admission to Harvard to a proactive outreach that required him to test key assumptions from his past through self-inquiry, and to stretch his definition of success by prototyping his career. Jack wasn't sure of his chances of admission (who really can be sure of admission to a Harvard PhD), but he motivated himself, and in some moments was willing to "burn the boats." He did the work, believed in himself, and got the prize.

What surprised us, I think, was Jack's final answer on what key tool actually was the keystone for him. Because, you see, Jack is a different person in many ways today. He argues his points differently. He listens more actively and checks with you to make sure he heard you right. He starts many responses with a thoughtful "hmm" that was never really there before, in our interactions at least. He affirms what others are saying. In short, he has become a more curious, resourceful (and humble) person even as his success has grown by leaps and bounds. For Jack, this all changed when he began to "go to the balcony"—a practice that was introduced in a previous chapter on emotions but bears repeating as one of the most effective techniques in self-coaching. "I stopped needing to be right all the time, when I could find a way to zoom out," he explains.

Professor William Ury at Harvard University is an expert in complex global negotiations. He works to bridge the divide between very angry people and parties, and has been screamed at by warlords and dictators. All that to say he gets the credit for really popularizing this message that we gain immense perspective and calm if we can zoom out a little bit, by "going to the balcony."

Imagine next time you are in a tough situation—someone is yelling at you or just called you out. Maybe you're finding yourself in a serious conversation and the anxiety is rising. Or you made a public mistake and you are starting to turn red in the face. All the equivalents of our ancestral sightings of a saber-toothed tiger.

In these moments, we can visualize ourselves going to a balcony, looking down at ourselves as if we were on stage below. *How interesting those characters look out there (and the acting isn't half bad either).* For some people, this practice of imagining yourself somewhere else in the middle of a conversation takes some practice, but Jack was able to work with it right away, and it has only improved for him since.

In "going to the balcony" and all the other self-work he has done, Jack has become more coach-like as well. Others have noticed it in big ways, and his narrative about himself has changed as a result. I suspect he will carry much of this with him for the rest of his leadership journey as he strives to establish his own lab or company in the future, and it all began with a few seconds of fresh perspective.

YOUR TURN

1. **Sixty Seconds of Breathing.** As introduced in the beginning of this chapter and in the young leader profile with Chris Bonnaig, this is my go-to strategy as you are walking into a meeting, preparing for a tough conversation, or calming down after a difficult encounter. All it takes is to notice the breath for sixty mindful seconds.

2. **Mindful Walking.** Again, for those who prefer more motion in their practice, you can take a walk and just notice the breeze, the trees, the ground, and the noise. Take in all the senses and really try to stay with the color and the smells. The Buddhists refer to this as "walking meditation," or *kinhin*, where movement through a beautiful landscape can deepen one's contemplation.[131]

---

131 Holiday, *Stillness is the Key*, 195 (describing also the important role of leisurely walking in the lives of luminaries such as Nikola Tesla, Ernest

3. **Loving Supporter.** This is an idea adapted from the work of Shakti Gawain and *Creative Visualization.* Imagine you are sitting across from a loving figure—it could be a relative or someone else who brings you great warmth and support. Imagine this person is showering love and praise upon you, and is overjoyed in giving this praise and love to you. Receive it and enjoy it. The Zen tradition also invites you to see yourself through the lens of a loving grandmother—someone who is biased in your favor and sees you as beautiful and lovable.[132]

4. **Loving-Kindness (*metta*).** There is one meditation practice that has been scientifically shown to improve empathy and compassion, and also combat compassion fatigue (for frontline health workers, for example). The idea is to find a time when it is appropriate for you to nourish others, and it requires you be at a certain baseline. All you do is imagine you are in the company of someone who you care deeply about and you are taking a ball of light that surrounds you, then slowly sharing that ball of light with your friend or loved one. *May they be happy, may they be healthy, may they be at peace and live with ease.* Then, you can extend that ball past you both to others in the area, and you repeat the same wish—*may they be happy, may they be healthy, may they be at peace and live with ease.* You can then expand the ball of light farther out to cover your own geographic area and beyond, to the whole continent and planet, as you continue the same

Hemingway, Charles Darwin, Daniel Kahneman, Martin Luther King, Jr., and Ulysses S. Grant, among others).

132 Chade-Meng Tan, *Search Inside Yourself: The Unexpected Path to Achieving Success, Happiness (and World Peace)* (New York: Harper Collins, 2012), 38.

wish that *may all beings be happy, may they be healthy, may they be at peace and live with ease.* This meditation is great for combating burnout.

"Muddy water, let stand, becomes clear."

-LAO TZE

Conclusion:
Self-Healing & More

---

*"You can't cross the sea merely by standing
and staring at the water."*

-RABINDRANATH TAGORE

I often ask people if they are "living the dream." The question usually evokes a smirk, and maybe a nervous chuckle from those who are unsure. Aren't we supposed to be living the dream?

Just ask my colleague doing reconciliation work in Darfur, Sudan, during a global pandemic whether we have things to be grateful for. Our time here is short, and I learned this the hard way when I saw family, friends, and acquaintances have their lives and dreams taken from them prematurely.

What will it really take to be "living the dream?"

When you serve yourself by reflecting on how core narratives and emotions shape your model of the world, you set the stage for a deeper exploration of what matters most. When we can define our more critical needs and build them into our daily or periodic planning processes, we ensure any further work is aligned with our core, which leads to greater personal fulfillment and better engagement and morale.

That alignment builds momentum for the deep work of self-coaching, and when the coaching works, we notice the incremental (or even sudden) shift into a more helpful place of self-healing.

When you are busy chipping away at the top of the iceberg, you are destined to an incremental "whack-a-mole" mentality that does not get to the core of the issue. As the saying goes, "No ship was sunk by the top of an iceberg."

What lies beneath is the real story (and danger) here, and this book consolidates some of the best available tools and frameworks so you can apply them just in time for them to be of true value. When you make those harder, larger changes under the surface, you create change that lasts.

As the late Jim Rohn said, "Everyone should make it their goal to earn a million dollars in their lifetime. Not for the money, that doesn't matter, but for who you become in the process." *Who you become.*

One easy-but-often-overlooked approach to discover the way forward is to sit with and "mine the gap" between your current state and your ideal state in any domain of your life.

Though this exercise can be challenging for clients to articulate, a savvy self-coach will find ways to dig in.

PROTOTYPING YOUR LIFE

Beyond tips for habit change, this book is also meant to give you a taste of what your life might be like in the future. Who is the ideal you, and how do you continue to explore that question? Your definition of success will make a difference here.

You can also take the time to imagine where you want to be in five years, build out a few alternatives, and then reach out to people who are living those alternate lives right now. In their book *Designing Your Life*, Bill Burnett and Dave Evans refer to this as prototyping your life.[133]

For me and many of my clients, prototyping our lives has been a huge gift in creating clarity and allowing for amazing possibilities. I am blessed with an incredible tribe of mentors who have helped me to pursue my ever-evolving dreams, and I know this to be the case for many successful young leaders around the world. The beauty of this prototyping mindset is you just cannot do this work alone—you do best when others are there to help you.

If you want to try it, I encourage you to reach out to people in your space who are several years ahead of you, and get their advice on whether they would recommend this path, what makes them happy in it, and what tips they might have

---

133 Bill Burnett and Dave Evans, *Designing Your Life: How to Build a Well-Lived, Joyful Life* (New York: Alfred A. Knopf, 2016), 103, 107–109.

for you. If I can be of help in this, do not hesitate to reach out to me as well.

WHY MOST DIETS FAIL

Marshall Goldsmith told me when *What Got You Here Won't Get You There* was the best business book of the year, the overall best-selling book that year was about dieting. "That diet book sold a heck of a lot more copies" than his book, he explained.

People buy those diet books and they just keep on buying them, because you cannot lose weight by reading. The act of purchasing and consuming does not yield any results. Diets also fail because people lose track, they forget, the environment exerts pressure and they get triggered in the wrong direction, motivation wanes because the purpose wasn't crystal clear, and maybe other needs or values win out. Diets fail for a number of these reasons and self-help efforts fail for the same reasons, in my opinion.

You can't coach yourself by reading a book either. Changing behavior is hard and it's an inside game that requires spark, structure, and support. That's why this book offers a menu—you choose from here or make your own, and you consume the content when you want, how you want. If you do the work, you will see the results.

CHOOSING FROM A MENU

Take a look, inspect, nibble a bit, or take a big bite. You will find your way as you usually do. I just emphasize there are no prescriptions or answers, per se, but rather options and ideas that have worked for others. What works for you is something you get to decide.

In their playful work *Crocodile Charlie and the Holy Grail*, John Kolm and Peter Ring tell us about a special (fictitious) meeting of wealthy investors and friends in Australia.[134] The group comes together periodically to discuss business ideas (mainly failures) and to work together for communal wealth. In one of these instances, the group is talking about the distinction between pedigree dogs and mongrels, as a metaphor for business principles. When it comes to building your business toolkit and acumen, it is tempting to buy someone else's ideas and models right off the shelf. *Let's purchase the well-pedigreed dog! It worked for them so it will work for me!* In most cases, "off the shelf" thinking will not work. It is far better to build your own "mongrel"—a hodgepodge of all the best there is out there that might work for you.

Again, the point is to choose from a menu, adapt the tools to fit your circumstances, and continue to iterate as you go.

ENJOYING EVERY STAGE OF THE TRAMPOLINE

Throughout our journey in this book, we talked about self-coaching as a supplement to, rather than a replacement for, formal coaching. I would really hope you use these skills to help you augment a coaching relationship. Most coaching clients miss the real value in between sessions.

---

134 John Kolm and Peter Ring, *Crocodile Charlie and the Holy Grail: How to Find Your Own Answers at Work and in Life* (New York: Penguin, 2003), 43–44.

I asked Michael Bungay Stanier, the number one thought leader in coaching in 2020, about his impression of coaching and self-coaching, and he offered a beautiful analogy of a trampoline. "I think the real coaching always happens between the sessions. A coaching session is like the moment you hit the trampoline. You hit the trampoline, you gain kinetic energy, and you spring again, but you wouldn't say trampolining only counts when you're on the trampoline. No, the whole thing is trampolining. And as you go up and you go down, that whole thing is coaching. The in-between thing is really important. If nothing happens between coaching sessions, it's not coaching. It's just random conversations every now and then," he explains.

So, avoid the random conversations, with your coach, with your friends, and with yourself. Spare yourself from mediocre. May you enjoy and benefit from the whole trampolining experience.

WISDOM LEAVES CLUES

Often, we are looking for wisdom in the wrong places, when we should be seeking out guides who have committed to a life of virtue, compassion, and service.

When Mark Zuckerberg needed advice on what to do with his fledgling company, Facebook, he approached Steve Jobs. Jobs suggested he go to India and meet a wise man named Neem Karoli Baba. This seemed strange advice to the young entrepreneur at the time, but he went. This mystic was known to be uncannily calm, happy at all times, and wise beyond his years (he was also incidentally unfazed by a very high dose of LSD). They say he radiated love—an unconditional love—that magnetized people to him. I picture Baba as the modern-day Oracle of Delphi, and his advice was said to have inspired an inflection point for Zuckerberg, who was then able to take Facebook to a whole new level.[135]

Neem Karoli Baba's work shows up in other important places and in the lives of several coaches and experts. Dr. Richard Alpert (Ram Dass) wrote about him in his book *Be Here Now*. Daniel Goleman and Tony Robbins also both speak of being deeply touched by Baba's influence.

It is important to find good archetypes and role models to learn from. Spiritual leaders such as Desmond Tutu, the Dalai Lama, Mother Teresa, and Neem Karoli Baba learned long ago what it would take to win on their own terms and transcend what holds many of us back. What might we learn from them?

---

135 Annie Gowen, "Inside the Indian Temple that Draws America's Tech Titans," *The Washington Post*, October 31, 2015.

Young Leader Profile: Mana Encourages Action

It is fitting to conclude our young leader profiles with Mana Kharrazi. Mana was a lead plaintiff on a lawsuit opposing Donald Trump's "Muslim Ban" in 2017, which meandered all the way to the US Supreme Court. She also helped lobby for new legislation to support human rights. Her name being on the paperwork meant she was not able to travel out of the country for fear of not being able to return. Tragically, she therefore wasn't there with her dad in Iran when he passed away. Some sacrifices take a depth of character and conviction that challenge our very nature of who we are and what we stand for. Mana is now head of rapid response coordination at Moveon.org and, truth be told, her background is just a litany of cause-driven activism on some of the most challenging and gut-wrenching social issues of our days. She should be an inspiration to all of us.

When I sat down to talk to her about how she achieved these things, self-coaching was an obvious theme. "As a child of immigrants with a lot of firsts (first time taking the SAT or going to school or launching a non-profit), I found I had to figure out those firsts on my own terms." This meant a heavy focus on journaling, using the mirror to rehearse big moments, finding time to breathe and practice self-care, and holding to her purpose of serving others.

Her advice to young leaders everywhere: "Be strategic. Be intentional about your personal and professional development. Know how to use your voice. Young people are way more anxious now than ever. It's about developing your attention span, paying attention to your social media consumption, and being able to leverage information to make better decisions. So many things culminated for this moment to be here, and it doesn't have to be all negative. You have potential to be visionary, to ask your elders for help, and to act with urgency. You have the potential and you have the power, and you should use it."

UNFINISHED BUSINESS

More needs to be done, of course. There is no "end" to any of this in sight for me either. Even as I write, I look forward to more physical activity, more efforts to reclaim calm, and new commitments to amplify the impact of self-coaching and the imprint of young leaders everywhere. What will it really take to get to our goals? It may even take everything we've got. I am committed to seeing it through, and I will be in our online community, learning from you and sharing my progress as well. Hope to see you there, where we are growing and serving together. We are never finished.

> *"Success is liking yourself, liking what you do,*
> *and liking how you do it."*
>
> —MAYA ANGELOU

Acknowledgments

A few words of appreciation...

To my great grandmother Biji who lived to be 102—for inspiration, humility, and the belief one can forgive, accept, and surrender in pursuit of a good life. I met you only once, but your life story informs mine every single day.

To my maternal grandparents Sukhdev and Kanta—both brilliant teachers—for the wisdom, the patience, the foresight, and the grace to leave everything you had in the "motherland" so others after you could be, do, and have so much more in America. I hope I grow up to be half as courageous or kind.

To my mother Uma, who (always) told me to stop working so hard and meant it, and to my aunt Alka who (generally) told me to work harder and meant it. I think you were both right, and I love you for it.

To my uncle Sanjeev, who first taught me about motivational thinking and "automobile university," and to my mentor and all-time favorite boss Cindy Mazur, for calling me into her office just to ask me to write this book. Big life decisions often need a nudge.

To my "newest parents" Ashok and Alka Khanna, for already carving out a spot in the study for my book to join the "family shelf," and to all of my family not otherwise listed, who both supported my journey and inspired me through theirs. I learn from all of you every day.

To my loving wife Ashima for her grace, as she made space and provided so much support for what must have felt like a decade of book writing. Any spouse of an author is indeed deserving of adulation, but I chose a particularly difficult time in our living history to take on this project. You shielded me from much of the worry and grief that might have overwhelmed me during the pandemic, starting on that fateful day when we left Istanbul on zero notice just as the world shut down. In retrospect, maybe I should have written this book some other time, but I sincerely hope our sacrifices help people.

To all those experts and young leaders who took out time to share their words of wisdom, their struggles, and their solutions, the world is better because of you.

To the rest of my care team, colleagues, beloved mentors, and "poor weather friends"—and the list is substantial—over the years, people have called me "self-made" or "bigger than my circumstances." You are that secret sauce.

To my "early adopters" and funding supporters, thank you for buying this book before it was even a book. You gave me the confidence (and created the necessary pressure) to get this thing done. I hope you read it, learn something from it, act on that learning, and amplify your impact as a result.

Thank you, Ajay and Neema Manaktala, Alex Chan, Alexandra Moore, Alka Aneja, Alyssa Brown, Ambuj and Anju Uppal, Angela Dash, Anik Sood, Anju Malik, Asha and Rajeev Saxena, Ashish and Meghan Khanna, Ashok and Alka Khanna, Ati Alipour, Atif Beg, Becci Crane, Benu Lahiry and Doug Tilley, Bina Patel, Brendan Pilver, Bryan Branon, Carlton Bruce, Carol Hoffman, Carol Mintz, Carolyn Skowron, Chad Ryerson, Charisse Williams, Charles Howard, Chintu and Monica Manuja, Chris Butsch, Christopher Bonnaig, Cindy Whitmoyer, Daisy Bugarin, Daniel Su, David Miller, David Pauker, Diana Carlson-Sherbo, Elisabeth Bissell, Elizabeth Hill, Elizabeth Stone, Eric Koester, Faraz Siddiqui and Laura Sander, Heather Sattler, Ike Kaludi, Inga Watkins, Jack Lindsay, Jae Lee and Chozin Oo, Jag Deo Lal, Janice Marie Johnson, Jay and Courtney Patel, Jeff Elkin, Jimmy Srun Jitender Sachdeva, Jon Moore, Josef Mitkevicius and Dioselina Carranco Gallardo, Jyoti Patel, Kahlill Palmer and Audrey Hsieh, Kellie Koford, Kelly Jackson, Kelvin and Senna Chung, Kunal Bhalla, LaToia Burkley, Laurie Mesibov, Lawrence Dudley, Linda Baron, Lindsay Pryor, Lorenzo Rodriguez-Olvera, Lucille Boettger, Madhu and Mahesh Chander, Maureen Kennedy, Melissa Alvarez Mangual, Michael and Jordana Nordlicht, Michael Hughes, Michelle Arbid, Mike Rozinsky, Mohib Qidwai and Zeibun Khan, Mozammel Hossain, Mrudula and Jashwant Shah, Mukesh and Anju Dang, Nancy and Dave Ross, Natalie

Fleury, Nausheen Ahmed and Saad Abbasi, Neetu and Gaurav Kumar, Nicholas Lovegrove, Nicole and Sushil Jain, Nitin Kailani, Noreen Razak, Odette Mucha and Matthew Klein, Patrick Chapman, Priya Jindal and Julius Duncan, Radhika and Hersh Shroff, Rama and Inder Sharma, Ravi and Amy Sharma, Ravi Mulani, Rea Wynder, Regina Duffey Moravek, Ripi Kohli and Ishu Chhabra, Rizwan Ahmad and Aminda Edgar, Robert Bibbiani, Robert Scott, Robin Dolobach, Roy Baroff, Rutvij Shanghavi and Punita Shroff, Sahil Aneja, Saleema Vellani, Sanjeev and Madhu Aneja, Sara Ehsani-Nia, Sarah and Jay Boyd, Sarah Kith, Scott Deyo, Serena Lee, Shawn and Elisa Gozarkhah, Shawn Hutchens, Shawn Shah and Melanie Oei, Sheila Weber, Sheily and Raju Panchal, Shyam and Natasha Toprani, Snigdha Gollamudi, Sophia Toh, Stacey Myers, Stephanie Fisher, Steven Knipfelberg, Steven Prevaux, Sunny Sassaman, Sydney Hoffman, Tamar Gur, Tara Thompson, Teresa Berry, Theresa Ford, Thomas Kosakowski, Thomas Tobin, Timothy Ruebke, Toi James, Towanna Burrous, Twinckle Patel, Victor Voloshin, Vijay and Anu Khurana, and Zeenia Irani.

To Eric Koester, the Creator Institute, New Degree Press, and my amazing editors there—Kristy Carter and Jordan Waterwash—among others, who helped breathe life into this project, and to my stellar book coaches Henry Devries and Marsha Sinetar for providing me the "top cover" I needed to build my vision without sacrificing my sanity. You made this possible—there is zero chance it would have happened without you.

What happens to a dream deferred? Sometimes it's worth the wait.

Thank you. Much love and gratitude to you all, and to all the others who have touched my life so far.

Appendix

——

Preface

2020 ICF Global Coaching Study: Executive Summary. Lexington, KY: International Coach Federation, 2020. https://coachfederation.org/app/uploads/2020/09/FINAL_ICF_GCS2020_ExecutiveSummary.pdf.

Brown, Brené. "Courage Over Comfort: Rumbling with Shame, Accountability, and Failure at Work." *Brené Brown* (blog), March 13, 2018. https://brenebrown.com/blog/2018/03/13/courage-comfort-rumbling-shame-accountability-failure-work/.

Clifton, Jim and Jim Harter, *It's the Manager: Moving from Boss to Coach.* New York: Gallup Press, 2019.

Stanier, Michael Bungay. "How to tame your Advice Monster." Filmed February 2020 at TEDxUniversityofNevada, Reno, Nevada. Video, 14:29. https://www.ted.com/talks/michael_bungay_stanier_how_to_tame_your_advice_monster.

Chapter 1

Adler, Mortimer and Charles Van Doren. *How to Read a Book.* New York: Simon and Schuster, 2014.

Eurich, Tasha. *Insight.* New York: Crown Business, 2017.

Feldman, David B. and Lee Daniel Kravetz. *Supersurvivors.* New York: HarperCollins Publishers Inc, 2014.

Schein, Edgar H. *Humble Inquiry: The Gentle Art of Asking Instead of Telling.* San Francisco, CA: Berrett-Koehler Publishers, 2013.

Search Inside Yourself Leadership Institute. "Search Inside Yourself Program." Accessed March 12, 2021. https://siyli.org/programs/search-inside-yourself.

TEDx Talks. "The Simple Formula that Builds Courage | Jaclyn DiGregorio | TEDxYouth@Berwyn." October 26, 2020. Video, 13:02. https://youtu.be/IitIgGHsPWw.

Webb, Caroline. *How to Have a Good Day.* New York: Crown Business, 2016.

Chapter 2

Barrett, Lisa Feldman. *Seven and a Half Lessons about the Brain.* New York: Houghton Mifflin Harcourt, 2020.

Bergland, Christopher. "Diaphragmatic Breathing Exercises and Your Vagus Nerve." *Psychology Today*, May 16, 2017. https://www.psychologytoday.com/intl/blog/the-athletes-way/201705/diaphragmatic-breathing-exercises-and-your-vagus-nerve.

Cuddy, Amy. "Your Body Language May Shape Who You Are."
Filmed June 2012 in Edinburgh, Scotland. TED video, 20:37.
https://www.ted.com/talks/amy_cuddy_your_body_language_
may_shape_who_you_are.

Dana, Deb. *Polyvagal Theory: Using the Autonomic Ladder to
Work with Perfectionism.* Mansfield, CT: The National Institute for the Clinical Application of Behavioral Medicine, 2018.
https://therapistuncensored.com/wp-content/uploads/2019/11/
NICABM-DebDana-PolyvagalTheoryUsingtheAutonomi-
cLaddertoWorkwithPerfectionism.pdf.

Ennenbach Matthias. *Buddhist Psychotherapy: A Guide for Beneficial Changes.* Twin Lakes, WI: Lotus Press, 2014.

Haidt, Jonathan. *The Happiness Hypothesis: Putting Ancient Wisdom to the Test of Modern Science.* New York: Basic Books,
2006.

Kross, Ethan. *Chatter: The Voice in Our Head and How to Harness
It.* New York: Random House, 2021.

Shetty, Jay. *Think Like a Monk: Train Your Mind for Peace and
Purpose Every Day.* New York: Simon and Schuster, 2020.

Streamer, Lindsey, Mark D. Seery, Cheryl L. Kondrak, Veronica
M. Lamarche, and Thomas L. Saltsman. "Not I but She: The
Beneficial Effects of Self-Distancing on Challenge/Thread
Cardiovascular Responses." *Journal of Experimental Social
Psychology* 70 (2017): 235–41.

Talks at Google. "Social Intelligence | Daniel Goleman." November 13, 2017. Video, 55:52. https://www.youtube.com/watch?v=-hoo_dIOP8k.

Tan, Chade-Meng. *Search Inside Yourself: The Unexpected Path to Achieving Success, Happiness (and World Peace).* New York: Harper Collins, 2012.

Thurman, Maxwell P. "Strategic Leadership." Presentation at The Strategic Leadership Conference, US Army War College, Carlisle Barracks, PA, 11 February 1991, cited in Mackey Sr., Richard H. *Translating Vision into Reality: The Role of the Strategic Leader.* Carlisle Barracks, PA: US Army War College, 1992. https://apps.dtic.mil/dtic/tr/fulltext/u2/a251129.pdf.

Webb, Caroline. *How to Have A Good Day: A Revolutionary Handbook for Work and Life.* New York: Crown, 2016.

Chapter 3

Daily Stoic. "A Stoic Response to Fear." Accessed February 22, 2021. https://dailystoic.com/stoic-response-fear/.

Ferriss, Timothy. "Why you Should Define your Fears Instead of your Goals." Filmed April 2017 in Vancouver, BC. TED video, 13:14.

Fowler, James H., and Nicholas A. Christakis. "Dynamic Spread of Happiness in a Large Social Network: Longitudinal Analysis over 20 Years in the Framingham Heart Study." *BMJ*, no. 337 (December 2008): a2338. https://doi.org/10.1136/bmj.a2338.

Fredrickson, Barbara L., and Marcial F. Losada. "Positive Affect and the Complex Dynamics of Human Flourishing." *American Psychologist* 60, no. 7 (2005): 678–86. https://doi. org/10.1037/0003-066x.60.7.678.

Kross, Ethan. *Chatter: The Voice in Our Head and How to Harness It.* New York: Random House, 2021.

Peterson, Christopher. "Discover the 'other' in yourself." In *The World Book of Happiness,* edited by Leo Bormans, 16–19. Singapore: Marshall Cavendish, 2011.

Peterson, Christopher. *A Primer in Positive Psychology.* Oxford: Oxford University Press, 2006.

Plutchik, Robert. "The Nature of Emotions: Human Emotions Have Deep Evolutionary Roots, a Fact That May Explain Their Complexity and Provide Tools for Clinical Practice." *American Scientist* 89, no. 4 (2001): 344–50.

Shetty, Jay. *Think Like a Monk: Train Your Mind for Peace and Purpose Every Day.* New York: Simon and Schuster, 2020.

Sieler, Alan. *Coaching to the Human Soul: Emotional Learning and Ontological Coaching* Vol. 2 of *Coaching to the Human Soul.* Blackburn North, Australia: Newfield Australia, 2003.

Spector, Nicole. "Smiling Can Trick Your Brain into Happiness — and Boost Your Health." *CNBC News,* November 28, 2017. https://www.nbcnews.com/better/health/smiling-can-trick-your-brain-happiness-boost-your-health-ncna822591

Ury, William. "The Walk from 'No' to 'Yes'." Filmed October 2010 in Chicago, IL. TED video, 18:30. https://www.ted.com/talks/william_ury_the_walk_from_no_to_yes?language=en.

Valham, Karin, Comp. *Extended Lam-Rim Outlines: Beginners' Meditation Guide.* Kathmandu, Nepal: Kopan Monastery, 2012.

Chapter 4

Daniel Simons. "The Monkey Business Illusion." April 28, 2010. Video, 1:41. https://www.youtube.com/watch?v=IGQmdoK_ZfY.

Méndez-Bértolo, Constantino, Stephan Moratti, Rafael Toledano, Fernando Lopez-Sosa, Roberto Martínez-Alvarez, Yee H. Mah, Patrik Vuilleumier, Antonio Gil-Nagel, and Bryan A. Strange. "A Fast Pathway for Fear in Human Amygdala." *Nature Neuroscience* 19, no. 8 (2016): 1041–9. https://doi.org/10.1038/nn.4324.

Olmeda, Rafael A., and John Marzulli. "Unarmed Amadou Diallo is Killed by Four Police Officers Who Shot at Him 41 Times in 1999." *New York Daily News*, February 3, 2015. https://www.nydailynews.com/new-york/unarmed-amadou-diallo-shot-killed-police-1999-article-1.2095255.

Scopelliti, Irene, Carey K. Morewedge, Erin McCormick, H. Lauren Min, Sophie Lebrecht, and Karim S. Kassam. "Bias Blind Spot: Structure, Measurement, and Consequences." *Management Science* 61, no. 10 (April 2015): 2468–86. https://doi.org/10.1287/mnsc.2014.2096.

Singer, Tania. "Understanding Others: Brain Mechanisms of Theory of Mind and Empathy." In *Neuroeconomics: Decision-Mak-*

ing and the Brain. Edited by Paul W. Glimcher, Ernst Fehr, Colin Camerer, and Russell Alan Poldrack, 251–68. Maryland Heights, MO: Academic Press, 2008.

Tan, Chade-Meng. *Search Inside Yourself: The Unexpected Path to Achieving Success, Happiness (and World Peace).* New York: Harper Collins, 2012.

Way Back. "How We Think Without Thinking: Malcolm Gladwell on Great Decision Makers (2005)." September 12, 2013. Video, 01:02:59. https://www.youtube.com/watch?v=bLxYpLXkiVU.

Chapter 5

Ali, Hira. *Her Way to the Top: The Glass Ceiling Is Thicker Than It Looks.* London, UK: Panoma Press, 2019. Kindle.

Arbinger Institute. *Leadership and Self-Deception: Getting Out of the Box.* Oakland, CA: Berrett-Koehler Publishers, 2002.

Arbinger Institute. *The Outward Mindset: Seeing Beyond Ourselves.* Oakland, CA: Berrett-Koehler Publishers, 2016.

Greenberg, Margaret H., and Senia Maymin. *Profit from the Positive: Proven Leadership Strategies to Boost Productivity and Transform Your Business.* New York: McGraw Hill Professional, 2013.

Kofman, Fred. *Conscious Business: How to Build Value Through Values.* Boulder, CO: Sounds True, 2006.

Lieberman, Matthew D., Naomi I. Eisenberger, Molly J. Crockett, Sabrina M. Tom, Jennifer H. Pfeifer, and Baldwin M. Way.

"Putting Feelings into Words: Affect Labeling Disrupts Amygdala Activity in Response to Affective Stimuli." *Psychological Science* 18, no. 5 (2007): 421–8.

Newell, Dave. "Growth Mindset: The Growth Leadership Series Part 2." *Chidsey Leadership Blog. Davidson College*, May 10, 2018. https://leadership.davidson.edu/leadership-experience/growth-mindset-the-growth-leadership-series-part-2/.

Petraeus, David. "Creator Institute Zoominar." Zoom webinar with Creator Institute, virtual, December 16, 2020.

Robbins, Tony. "Why We Do What We Do." Filmed February 2006 in Monterey, CA. TED video, 21:33. https://www.ted.com/talks/tony_robbins_why_we_do_what_we_do

Twist, Lynne. *The Soul of Money: Transforming Your Relationship with Money and Life*. New York: W. W. Norton & Company, 2017.

Chapter 6

Geirland, John. "Go with The Flow." *Wired*, September 1, 1996. https://www.wired.com/1996/09/czik/. Cited in Tan,

Chade-Meng. *Search Inside Yourself: The Unexpected Path to Achieving Success, Happiness (and World Peace)*. New York: Harper Collins, 2012.

Godin, Seth. *The Dip: A Little Book That Teaches You When to Quit (and When to Stick)*. New York: Portfolio, 2007.

Newport, Cal. *Deep Work: Rules for Focused Success in a Distracted World*. New York: Grand Central Publishing, 2016.

Powell, Colin, and Joe Montana. Get Motivated Workbook. Tampa, FL: Get Motivated Seminars, 2010.

Shetty, Jay. *Think Like a Monk: Train Your Mind for Peace and Purpose Every Day*. New York: Simon and Schuster, 2020.

Tan, Chade-Meng. *Search Inside Yourself: The Unexpected Path to Achieving Success, Happiness (and World Peace)*. New York: Harper Collins, 2012.

TEDx Talks. "How to Take Better Care of Your Brain Using M.E.S.H. | Chris Butsch | TEDxWaltonHigh." March 27, 2019. Video, 17:48. https://www.youtube.com/watch?v=LBMkr52M-mog.

TEDx Talks. "Post-Traumatic Gifted: Moving from Scarcity to Abundance - Russell Redenbaugh at TEDxBend." May 22, 2013. video, 18:00. https://youtu.be/AOOc3VO_Gyg.

Thakura, Bhaktivonada. "The Nectarean Instructions of Lord Caitanya." *Hari Kirtan*, June 12, 2010.

Chapter 7

Carroll, Lewis. *Alice's Adventures in Wonderland*. New York: Macmillan, 1920.

Easwaran, Eknath, Trans. *Bhagavad Gita*. Tomales, CA: Nilgiri Press, 2007.

Ferriss, Tim. "Naval Ravikant." June 4, 2020. In *Tools of Titans*. Podcast, audio, 16:33. https://anchor.fm/tools-of-titans/episodes/Naval-Ravikant-efo4no.

Friedman, Shlomit. "Priming Subconscious Goals." In *New Developments in Goal Setting and Task Performance*, edited by Edwin A. Locke and Gary P. Latham. New York: Routledge, 2013.

Harvard School of Public Health. Harvard Program on Refugee Trauma (website). Accessed February 22, 2021. http://hprt-cambridge.org.

Hyatt, Michael, and Daniel Harkavy. *Living Forward: A Proven Plan to Stop Drifting and Get the Life You Want*. Grand Rapids, MI: Baker Books, 2016.

Jeb Corliss. "Grinding the Crack." August 22, 2011. Video, 3:29. https://www.youtube.com/watch?v=TWfph3iNC-k.

Kaufman, Scott Barry. *Transcend: The New Science of Self-Actualization*. New York: TarcherPerigee, 2020.

Maslow, Abraham Harold. "A Theory of Human Motivation." *Psychological Review* 50, no. 4 (1943): 370–396.

Murphy, Mark. "Neuroscience Explains Why You Need to Write Down Your Goals If You Actually Want to Achieve Them." *Forbes*, April 15, 2018.

https://www.forbes.com/sites/markmurphy/2018/04/15/neuroscience-explains-why-you-need-to-write-down-your-goals-if-you-actually-want-to-achieve-them/#655b5fc77905

Robbins, Tony. "Why We Do What We Do." Filmed February 2006 in Monterey, CA. TED video, 21:33. https://www.ted.com/talks/tony_robbins_why_we_do_what_we_do

Robbins, Tony. *Personal Power*. Read by author. Santa Monica, CA: Guthy-Renker, 1996. Audio DVD.

Schwartz, Peter. *The Art of the Long View*. New York: Currency Doubleday, 1996.

Shetty, Jay. *Think Like a Monk: Train Your Mind for Peace and Purpose Every Day*. New York: Simon and Schuster, 2020.

Stafford, Tom. "Your Subconscious is Smarter Than You Might Think." *BBC*, February 18, 2015. https://www.bbc.com/future/article/20150217-how-smart-is-your-subconscious.

Traumatology Institute. "Charles R. Figley, PhD." Accessed February 22, 2021. https://tulanetraumatologyinstitute.com/charles-figley

Chapter 8

Baikie, Karen A., and Kay Wilhelm. "Emotional and Physical Health Benefits of Expressive Writing." *Advances in Psychiatric Treatment* 11, no. 5 (2005): 338–46.

Cuddy, Amy. "Your Body Language May Shape Who You Are." Filmed June 2012 in Edinburgh, Scotland. TED video, 20:37. https://www.ted.com/talks/amy_cuddy_your_body_language_may_shape_who_you_are.

Ferriss, Tim. "What My Morning Journal Looks Like." *The Tim Ferriss Show*, January 15, 2015. https://tim.blog/2015/01/15/morning-pages/.

Ferriss, Timothy. *Tools of Titans: The Tactics, Routines, and Habits of Billionaires, Icons, and World-class Performers*. New York: Houghton Mifflin Harcourt, 2017.

Hay, Louise. *Mirror Work: 21 Days to Heal Your Life*. Carlsbad, CA: Hay House, 2016.

Holiday, Ryan. *Stillness is the Key*. New York: Portfolio/Penguin, 2019.

Jimrohnfan. "Jim Rohn - Five Major Pieces to the Life Puzzle Masterclass." June 11, 2020. Video, 50:25. https://www.youtube.com/watch?v=_kapNWjgHVM.

Kelly, Anita E., and Kevin J. McKillop. "Consequences of Revealing Personal Secrets." *Psychological Bulletin* 120, no. 3 (1996): 450–65.

Klein, Kitty, and Adriel Boals. "Expressive Writing can Increase Working Memory Capacity." *Journal of Experimental Psychology: General* 130, no. 3 (2001): 520–33.

Pasricha, Neil. *You Are Awesome: How to Navigate Change, Wrestle with Failure, and Live an Intentional Life*. Toronto, Canada: Simon and Schuster, 2019.

Peale, Norman Vincent. *Positive Imaging*. New Delhi: Orient Paperbacks, 2006.

Pennebaker, James W., and John Frank Evans, *Expressive Writing: Words that Heal*. Washington: Idyll Arbor, 2014.

Peterson, Christopher. *A Primer in Positive Psychology*. Oxford: Oxford University Press, 2006.

Sapadin, Linda. "Talking to Yourself: A Sign of Sanity." *Psych Central*, December 7, 2012. https://psychcentral.com/blog/talking-to-yourself-a-sign-of-sanity.

Shetty, Jay. *Think Like a Monk: Train Your Mind for Peace and Purpose Every Day*. New York: Simon & Schuster, Inc, 2020.

Tan, Chade-Meng. *Search Inside Yourself: The Unexpected Path to Achieving Success, Happiness (and World Peace)*. New York: Harper Collins, 2012.

Well, Tara. *Mirror Meditation*. 2020. https://www.mirrormeditation.com.

Zetlin, Minda. "Steve Jobs Asked Himself One Question Every Day. You Should Too." *INC*, July 31, 2015. https://www.inc.com/minda-zetlin/steve-jobs-asked-himself-one-question-every-day-you-should-too.html.

Chapter 9

Bormans, Leo, ed. *The World Book of Love*. Tielt, Belgium: Lannoo Publishers, 2014.

CNN. "Rumsfeld / Knowns." April 1, 2016. Video, 0:26. https://www.youtube.com/watch?v=REWeBzGuzCc.

Kirk, Jeremy, Anita MacDonald, Paul Lavender, Jessica Dean, and Gretchen Rubin. "Can Treatment Adherence Be Improved by Using Rubin's Four Tendencies Framework to Understand a Patient's Response to Expectations." *Biomedicine Hub* 2, no. 2 (2017): 1–12.

Luft, Joseph, and Harry Ingham. "The Johari Window: A Graphic Model of Interpersonal Awareness." Paper presented at the Proceedings of the Western Training Laboratory in Group Development, University of California, Los Angeles, 1955.

Rock, David. "SCARF: A Brain-Based Model for Collaborating with and Influencing Others." *NeuroLeadership Journal* 1, no. 1 (2008): 44–52.

Rubin, Gretchen. *The Four Tendencies: The Indispensable Personality Profiles That Reveal How to Make Your Life Better (and Other People's Lives Better, Too).* New York: Harmony Books, 2017.

vladimerk1. "Capuchin Monkey Fairness Experiment." April 13, 2012. Video, 0:57. https://www.youtube.com/watch?v=-KSry-JXDpZo.

Chapter 10

Ferriss, Timothy. *Tools of Titans: The Tactics, Routines, and Habits of Billionaires, Icons, and World-class Performers.* New York: Houghton Mifflin Harcourt, 2017.

Gawain, Shakti. *Creative Visualization: Use the Power of Your Imagination to Create What You Want in Your Life.* Novato, CA: Nataraj Publishing, 2002.

Goleman, Daniel, and Richard J. Davidson. *Altered Traits: Science Reveals How Meditation Changes Your Mind, Brain, and Body.* New York: Avery, 2017.

Holiday, Ryan. *Stillness is the Key.* New York: Portfolio/Penguin, 2019.

Kabat-Zinn, Jon. *Wherever You Go, There You Are: Mindfulness Meditation for Everyday Life.* London: Piatkus, 1994.

Mejia, Zameena. "A Stanford Expert Explains How Meditation Helped the Thai Boys Survive." *CNBC*, July 10, 2018. https://www.cnbc.com/2018/07/10/stanford-expert-explains-how-meditation-helped-the-thai-boys-survive.html.

Narayana. *The Hitopadesa.* Translated by A. N. D. Haksar. New York: Penguin Classics, 2007.

Shetty, Jay. *Think Like a Monk: Train Your Mind for Peace and Purpose Every Day.* New York: Simon & Schuster, Inc, 2020.

Tan, Chade-Meng. *Search Inside Yourself: The Unexpected Path to Achieving Success, Happiness (and World Peace).* New York: Harper Collins, 2012.

Tim Ferriss. "Tony Robbins Interview: Part 1 (Full Episode) | The Tim Ferriss Show (Podcast)." October 30, 2015. Video, 1:08:30. https://www.youtube.com/watch?v=A7jOqYWJUKg.

Conclusion

Burnett, Bill, and Dave Evans. *Designing Your Life: How to Build a Well-Lived, Joyful Life.* New York: Alfred A. Knopf, 2016.

Gowen, Annie. "Inside the Indian Temple that Draws America's Tech Titans." *The Washington Post*, October 31, 2015. https://www.washingtonpost.com/world/asia_pacific/ inside-the-indian-temple-that-draws-americas-tech-titans/2015/10/30/03b646d8-7cb9-11e5-bfb6-65300a5ff562_story. html.

Kolm, John, and Peter Ring. *Crocodile Charlie and the Holy Grail: How to Find Your Own Answers at Work and in Life.* New York: Penguin, 2003.

CPSIA information can be obtained
at www.ICGtesting.com
Printed in the USA
BVHW041949071021
618413BV00003B/8

9 781636 768076